COMFORT OF THE SCRIPTURES

Exhortational Themes
based on the
Daily Readings

COMFORT
of the
SCRIPTURES

Exhortational Themes
based on the
Daily Readings

HARRY TENNANT

THE CHRISTADELPHIAN
404 SHAFTMOOR LANE
HALL GREEN
BIRMINGHAM B28 8SZ

2006

First Published 2006

ISBN 0 85189 171 3

Cover Picture:
Portmore Loch, Moorfoot Hills, West Lothian, Scotland
Photograph and calligraphy:
Courtesy of Paul Wasson

Printed in England by:

THE CROMWELL PRESS
TROWBRIDGE
WILTSHIRE
BA14 0XB

CONTENTS

v

PREFACE

B ROTHER Harry Tennant was known to thousands of brethren and sisters all round the world. From his regular visits to distant parts he was known as an enthralling and motivational speaker, and through his writings as a clear and logical thinker with an ability to convey profound thoughts in elevated language. Yet no one who knew him as either a speaker or writer believed him to be a distant figure; he was eminently approachable, and helped very many by his discreet and scriptural counsel. The personal loss felt by so many at his passing reflects Brother Harry's interest in and concern for each individual: he had a remarkable memory for the names, faces and circumstances of the numerous brethren and sisters he met on his travels.

This interest in people was seen also in his love of Bible characters. When he spoke or wrote about Moses or David, it was as if he knew them individually. Above all, he sought to know his Lord, and always spoke eloquently about him.

He spoke openly and frankly about the difficulties of living as a disciple of Christ in today's world. He grieved over the pressures that the young have to face, and constantly advised them to draw closer to the Lord Jesus and the Father through prayer, through daily Bible reading and through ecclesial fellowship with brethren and sisters. His own strong marriage gave him a sound base from which to encourage those who faced difficulties in their own relationships. He offered practical solutions for daily problems, and always encouraged his hearers to strive for the mark of the high calling in Christ Jesus.

Brother Harry fell asleep in Christ on May 31, 2004. Among his papers, he left a message to be read at his funeral. It is appropriate to include part of it as his final word of exhortation:

> "Remember that there is no joy like the joy of the Truth, no hope like the Hope of Israel, and no comfort like the peace of God which passes all understanding. Hold fast to the word of life; live the life of full service to God; shun all that is not pure and wholesome; keep faith with Christ Jesus our Lord and with one another, and with the Lord God our Father who will bless you abundantly above all that you can ask or think. Remember, the best is yet to come! Fare ye well."

MICHAEL ASHTON
Birmingham, 2006

FOREWORD

IT would be an unusual Breaking of Bread service: but if the exhorter could imagine an audience consisting of some brethren and sisters who were hungry, some who were sick, some cold, some badly clothed, and almost all travel-soiled after a week's journey, he would find his compassion stirred. In fact the company of brethren and sisters is just like that. Such is our spiritual state as we repair to the table of the Lord to find food for our souls, healing for the mind, warmth from fellowship with kindred spirits, clothing for the journey through life and bathing from the stains of a week's contact with the world. It is to these that the word is ministered and the task is made more real and urgent by looking in through the windows of the minds of our fellow-partakers.

Does the word of exhortation help any of these? "If a son shall ask bread of any of you that is a father, will he give him a stone? ... Or if he shall ask an egg, will he offer him a scorpion?" The questions are from the Master. What then of our answers, brethren? Is our word of exhortation bread or stones, eggs or scorpions?

Listen again. "I was an hungered, and ye gave me meat: I was thirsty, and ye gave me drink: I was a stranger, and ye took me in: naked, and ye clothed me: I was sick, and ye visited me: I was in prison, and ye came unto me." Such is the scene from judgement. It is most appropriate to the word in need spoken by the true exhorter. Is our word like that? Is it designed to be like that – do we intend it to be?

No exhortation, however cleverly composed, has served its true purpose if it has failed to enter into the feelings of the hearers by showing true sympathy and compassion.

The word of exhortation is no set speech, no display of oratory, no occasion for self-preening or exhibition of a good memory or a discerning taste for good English. The world has enough of that. Rather is it that "through **comfort of the scriptures** we might have hope". Let the brother seek to follow Paul in his words when he "exhorted them all that with purpose of heart they would cleave unto the Lord": follow him in his true service for Christ when he comforted "the souls of the disciples and exhorted them to continue in the faith". Such is exhortation: not merely what is spoken but what it is hoped to achieve.

It is good to have in one's mind in preparing exhortation certain basic ideas behind the very word "exhortation" itself: comfort, consolation, beseeching, urging others forward by encouragement at their ear and elbow.

Sometimes one hears the brother appointed to exhort bemoaning the fact and saying that he cannot find something worthwhile to say. Perhaps a word or two in this direction will be of help.

Acceptable matter for exhortation rarely comes out of the blue. Inspiration and genius are not the key. Four things are necessary: God's exhortations – His living word designed for our very need and revealing itself to the meditative, regular reader; prayer – he who learns to lean upon a sympathetic Mediator in heaven will acquire a similar spirit toward others; self-examination – let the exhorter examine himself, ferret out his every need and ask himself what would a good exhortation perform in him; an awareness of others – fellowship revealing itself in being conscious of the joys and sorrows, trials and triumphs, pitfalls and upward helps of the many kinds of brethren and sisters. The quality of the good wine of exhortation is then sealed by careful preparation.

What then of the theme for our exhortation? Many brethren make it an invariable rule to find the word in the readings for the day. This has many advantages. The brethren and sisters have companied with one another through some or all of the readings for the week and have absorbed some of the atmosphere of the allotted portions. They are prepared to go on from there. The presiding brother, too, will have considered the readings in setting the pattern of the hymns and prayers. Thus exhortation based on the readings for the day tends to give unity to the whole meeting and to spread out its roots among the waters of our common reading of the word, thereby taking advantage of one of the unique marks of our community.

There are, however, occasions when such an exhortation consists of bits and pieces because it tries to find something from each reading, and, sometimes strains credulity by finding a common theme when one scarcely exists.

Whether by this means or by another it is certain that an exhortation is made memorable by having a clear and helpful theme. Notice how Jesus took advantage of this fact when he spoke of light, of the vine, of bread, of water, of the word. Each theme came alive in his hands by simple development and careful repetition. The homely illustration and uncomplicated presentations with abundant allusion to the written word of God made ordinary people who had problems and cares take note and find help.

The scriptures abound with themes as anthills are alive with ants: and the themes will work as industriously and unitedly as ants in their tasks. Get hold of a good theme. It has not to abound in involved exposition, though it will make clear the word of God, but it must go to the root of faith and life, hope and experience, trial and steadfastness. Remember the hungry, the sick, the poor, the cold and those in tattered clothing. Seek to be of service at some cost to yourself. Prepare your exhortation with practical ends in your mind. We fail by imagining that skilful, well-composed talks are the key to this matter – they are not. The key is our sympathetic handling of the word of God in the service of men and women on the way to eternal life. Keep them in mind and help them. See Christ ever moving among them in his tireless endeavour to bring and to keep sheep in the pasture of God.

One of the current dangers in religion around us is that the kind of help that a psychologist or psychiatrist can give, or the wisdom of plain common sense, is taking the place of the wholesome word of God. It is undoubtedly possible to obtain help from these sources – one sees it in men and women around us – but it is not the help whereby a man may inherit immortality. True exhortation must come right out of God's mind by His word into ours by hearing. It is altogether different from the moralising in which humanists without Christ can freely indulge. Let us not be beguiled – or try to beguile others – by sweet appealing words about being good men and true. We are not to be good men only, we are to be new men – and only God can produce those: we are not to be merely truthful but men of the Truth – God's Truth as revealed by Him.

Unless words of exhortation reverberate with the themes of the kingdom of God, of the redemption of dying men by the death of the Son of God, of the return of the King and the day of resurrection and judgement and of the need for being watchful in a sinful world, we are missing the mark. Only the constant re-echoing of the words of scripture will keep us from the hidden traps of a world which is making so broad its morals of goodness that they will embrace almost every religion and way of life provided that they have a good social conscience and a heightened sense of unselfishness.

We are being exhorted to higher things: not simply the purifying of ordinary men by ennobling virtues of man's devising but by transformation of the sons of men into the sons of God. "But exhort one another daily, while it is called Today; lest any of you be hardened through the deceitfulness of sin. For we are made partakers of Christ, if we hold (fast, RV) the beginning of our confidence stedfast unto the end." Great things indeed. Partakers of Christ!

Occasion will arise when the exhorting brother must meet special needs – death's sudden visit, a baptism and receiving into fellowship, and many other circumstances which affect the thinking of the meeting. Let him give thought to these things. There need be no eulogising of personalities – no unnecessary and prolonged praising of dead men, for example – but the turning of the mind to the abundant **comfort of the scriptures** where the common destiny of mankind is clear and the unique hope of the believer is made plain. Meet the needs of the moment with an open Bible.

There are occasions when the exhorter should be silent on certain matters. He should never make the platform a place for firing shots in some ecclesial controversy or –

worse still – direct his words at some one individual in the meeting. He is an exhorter and should strengthen the ecclesia. True he will sometimes sound a clarion call, a warning in times of danger, but he will not pronounce judgement on members of the ecclesia. There is another who shall do that.

May a word be said here about the choice of subjects for fraternal exhortations? These are by far easier to deal with if they are scriptural, and free from complications if the two or three subjects are not so related as to be inseparable. Pity the speaker who has to practise gymnastics to prevent obtruding upon the theme of a following speaker!

An exhorting brother will always exhort himself. He will find his own weaknesses and try to overcome them, thereby helping others: he will sink his pride, and remember his office is that of a servant and not a ruler or a judge: he will remember his Master and be duly reverent: he will remember his daily living and seek to be a worthy bearer of tidings to his brethren.

"Ye know how we exhorted and comforted and charged every one of you, as a father doth his children, that ye would walk worthy of God, who hath called you unto his kingdom and glory. For this cause also thank we God without ceasing, because, when ye received the word of God which ye heard of us, ye received it not as the word of men, but as it is in truth, the word of God, which effectually worketh also in you that believe."

Servants of the Lord (chapter 7)

1

BEGINNING AND NEW
1st January

Genesis 1,2　　　　Psalms 1,2　　　　**Matthew 1,2**

WITH the start of each new year comes the joy of beginning again the reading of the Bible. Our daily readings bring us to the start of things and urge us to renew our allegiance to God. This is when, the world over, irrespective of religious affiliation, men and women make resolutions, 'promises' that they will do this or that, or stop doing this or that. There is something about human nature that likes things that are new; new books, new clothes, new experiences, new friends.

It is only the Bible that gives us the best of everything. Within its pages can be found the complete and only explanation of the beginnings of things, and promises of things yet to come.

Genesis

"In the beginning God created the heaven and the earth."　　　　　　　　　　　　　　　　(Genesis 1:1)

This is not the beginning of God, for He has no beginning and no ending. He is from everlasting to everlasting. This verse explains to us how all things came into existence. It tells us that God made them – God created them. He only is the Creator, and things were not made out of nothing. They were made out of God's Spirit:

"By the word of the LORD were the heavens made; and all the host of them by the breath of his mouth."　　　　　　　　　　　　　　　　　　　　　　　(Psalm 33:6)

The record goes on to show that it was a very good world. It was "very good" for the purpose for which God made it. The phrase does not mean that it was perfect or complete, because Adam and Eve had not yet developed their characters. They were placed in God's world on probation. They were there on test, to be proved – and they failed. God's new beginning, His fresh creation, was smudged but not frustrated. Man had failed, but God's

1

plan would succeed. His purpose would yet be fulfilled by a new beginning in the promised seed:

"And God said, Let us make man in our image, after our likeness: and let them have dominion over the fish of the sea, and over the fowl of the air, and over the cattle, and over all the earth, and over every creeping thing that creepeth upon the earth." (Genesis 1:26)

Psalm 8 and Hebrews 2 tell us that this verse was not fulfilled when God made Adam and Eve, but that it looked down the long road of human history to its fulfilment through the Lord Jesus Christ.

The New Man

"The book of the generation of Jesus Christ, the son of David, the son of Abraham." (Matthew 1:1)

"Generation" reminds us of "Genesis". The two words have the same meaning: 'origin' or 'beginning'. Here was the first man of a new generation, a new beginning, the generation of the righteous:

"A seed shall serve him; it shall be accounted to the Lord for a generation. They shall come, and shall declare his righteousness unto a people that shall be born, that he hath done this." (Psalm 22:30,31)

"This shall be written for the generation to come: and the people which shall be created shall praise the LORD." (Psalm 102:18)

"Yet it pleased the LORD to bruise him; he hath put him to grief: when thou shalt make his soul an offering for sin, he shall see his seed, he shall prolong his days, and the pleasure of the LORD shall prosper in his hand." (Isaiah 53:10)

"Therefore if any man be in Christ, he is a new creature: old things are passed away; behold, all things are become new." (2 Corinthians 5:17)

A New Beginning

As man's history progresses and we come eventually to learn about the kingdom of God it looks as though it is too late. Sins press so heavily upon mankind that we feel the kingdom cannot be for us. But, of course, the joy that is revealed to us in the word of God is that anyone can have a new beginning. By faith and baptism the past is blotted out and we come from the waters of baptism as newborn babes. It is as though a great burden has been lifted from our shoulders. We are new men and women in Christ. We have a new page, a new book, in which to write:

"Therefore we are buried with him by baptism into death: that like as Christ was raised up from the dead by the glory of the Father, even so we also should walk in newness of life. For if we have been planted together in the likeness of his death, we shall be also in the likeness of his resurrection: knowing this, that our old man is crucified with him, that the body of sin might be destroyed, that henceforth we should not serve sin. For he that is dead is freed from sin."   (Romans 6:4-7)

The New Testament

This wonder is wrought by the death of Christ. At the last supper he said:

"For this is my blood of the new testament, which is shed for many for the remission of sins."

(Matthew 26:28)

A new covenant in Christ.

It is a covenant that places us on the road to eternal life: the covenant of the forgiveness of sins and of promise. The old covenant was the covenant made with Israel at Sinai. It was the covenant of fire, thunder, lightning and the sound of a trumpet; a covenant given at the hand of angels. By a supreme paradox, the new covenant in Christ is older than the old covenant:

"And this I say, that the covenant, that was confirmed before of God in Christ, the law, which was four hundred and thirty years after, cannot disannul, that it should make the promise of none effect."

(Galatians 3:17)

The new covenant is that in which the saints from Abel onwards have been bound, it is the covenant of redemption and of hope of life eternal.

A New Commandment

The hallmark of the new covenant is the relationship between those who are in Christ. The selfless love he displayed for their salvation is to become their motivation:

3

"A new commandment I give unto you, That ye love one another; as I have loved you, that ye also love one another." (John 13:34)

"And above all these things put on love, which is the bond of perfectness." (Colossians 3:14)

This is the crown of our spiritual life, the means by which everything is held together, the indispensable quality without which all of the others prove to be useless and in vain.

Some regard love as a lesser, a weaker quality and would wish to set alongside it strong words like 'defending the truth', or 'holding fast to the faith'. The fact is that love is the means by which everything has been accomplished; it is the driving force which sent Jesus into the world and by which he was victorious. Love is both the beginning and the end; it is the cause and means of our salvation, creating new beings energised by love.

"Herein is love, not that we loved God, but that he loved us, and sent his Son to be the propitiation for our sins." (1 John 4:10)

Our Response

If we were to regard our response as the necessary performance of a duty, or as keeping the commandments, we would be running the risk of creating for ourselves a law of salvation by works. If, on the other hand, we were to seek to bring forth the fruit of the Spirit we would be on entirely different ground:

"But the fruit of the Spirit is love, joy, peace, longsuffering, gentleness, goodness, faith, meekness, temperance ..." (Galatians 5:22,23)

These things rise higher than the mere routine of keeping the law, and they know no limits:

"Many waters cannot quench love, neither can the floods drown it." (Song of Solomon 8:7)

Once this kind of love – Christlike love – suffuses all that we do in every walk of life, then life takes on a new and beautiful nature.

But most important of all, there are new things to come in God's purpose:

4

"Nevertheless we, according to his promise, look for new heavens and a new earth, wherein dwelleth righteousness."　　　　　　　　　(2 Peter 3:13)

"He that hath an ear, let him hear what the Spirit saith unto the churches; To him that overcometh will I give to eat of the hidden manna, and will give him a white stone, and in the stone a new name written, which no man knoweth saving he that receiveth it."
(Revelation 2:17)

"And they sung a new song, saying, Thou art worthy to take the book, and to open the seals thereof: for thou wast slain, and hast redeemed us to God by thy blood out of every kindred, and tongue, and people, and nation; and hast made us unto our God kings and priests: and we shall reign on the earth."
(Revelation 5:9,10)

"And he that sat upon the throne said, Behold, I make all things new. And he said unto me, Write: for these words are true and faithful."　　(Revelation 21:5)

Each time we meet around the emblems is an opportunity to recall the new beginning when we entered into Christ. The bread and wine are tokens of the new covenant and remind us powerfully of the new commandment. Let this day, this week, this year be one of renewed commitment, as we await the great new day of the Lord.

COMFORT OF THE SCRIPTURES

2

AND THE RAINS CAME
4th January

Genesis 7,8   **Psalms 9,10**   **Matthew 6**

THE old man had died. He was the oldest man who had ever lived. His father was a prophet and had given him a name of intent and of meaning: 'Missile of death' or 'When he dies, it shall come'. His father Enoch had said that judgement would come:

"Behold, the Lord cometh with ten thousands of his saints, to execute judgment upon all, and to convince all that are ungodly among them of all their ungodly deeds which they have ungodly committed, and of all their hard speeches which ungodly sinners have spoken against him." (Jude verses 14,15)

The rains came

There had been a strange procession of animals and finally of men entering the great wooden boat which Noah had built, and for seven days they had remained inside. And then it began to rain – torrential and unrelenting rain. Every river and stream broke its banks. Water broke out from beneath in unbelievable quantities.

At first men sheltered indoors and then made for higher ground, and higher still. They were drenched. The animals sought refuge until those that had not died in the rising and falling water were driven to the highest points of refuge. Food supplies were cut off. It rained without intermission day and night, day and night.

The Ark was afloat, but there was no way in. Even had they been able to reach the door they would not have succeeded, because God had shut Noah in. Perhaps some thought of the message and life of Noah, but it was too late. Remorse was no substitute for repentance, and it was too late for that.

For those who survived so long, the highest hills and mountains were soon sinking below the water. The tempestuous waters provided no refuge. Even had people

7

managed to cling to wreckage or find something more substantial on which to float, it was useless because there was no food, and it rained forty days and forty nights. And the flood prevailed one hundred and fifty days.

All this took place over 1,600 years from the day when Adam was made. One family survived by the grace of God. They survived by faith in the word of God and a life which was righteous, and by doing works of faith – building an Ark and entering in with the animals which God had caused to assemble.

A Parable of Redemption

It was a parable of the way to eternal life. There is only One Family and One Ark. We are assembled today as part of that family who have taken refuge in Christ the Ark, pitched within and without. We are in the nests in the Ark with light from above through the windows of the word.

Our world is like their world. It is filled with self-indulgence and violence. Men are corrupt. Evil imaginations are within and portrayed on screens without. Evil imaginations are lived out in daily life.

Judgement Day

This is the theme of all three of our daily readings. Judgement is at the beginning of Genesis, the beginning of the Psalms and the beginning of Matthew. Judgement is not to be ignored. There will be a day of account, a day of reckoning, a day of truth:

"But the LORD shall endure for ever: he hath prepared his throne for judgment. And he shall judge the world in righteousness, he shall minister judgment to the people in uprightness." (Psalm 9:7,8)

"Lay not up for yourselves treasures upon earth, where moth and rust doth corrupt, and where thieves break through and steal: but lay up for yourselves treasures in heaven, where neither moth nor rust doth corrupt, and where thieves do not break through nor steal: for where your treasure is, there will your heart be also." (Matthew 6:19-21)

Beginnings make endings

There was nothing surprising about the judgement which God brought on Noah's world, except the nature of it. It deserved nothing better. A year's beginnings, a life's beginnings, a marriage's beginnings, a career's beginnings all have the seeds of the future within them. There is nothing surprising about them, except the nature of the future. The kind of future is made by the kind of present we make. Of course, as in the days of Noah, God grants us time for renewal, for repentance, a time to change course. The nature of the past determines in some measure whether we shall be able to take those opportunities. The people in Noah's day were too far along the road to destruction to find it in themselves to turn back. Not even the uprightness of Noah and the evidence of the vessel growing day by day to completion, and the prophecy of Enoch and the living and dying prophecy of Methuselah could turn their hearts. The lesson is that there is a time for repentance, and a time when it can be too late.

Noah's salvation was not an instantaneous matter; it took time. In the first place, God had to make known to him the way, and to command Noah to take it. Noah had to listen and obey. His salvation depended on what he believed and on what he did. Salvation is not possible unless we do something in response to the word and command of God.

The Warnings in Ecclesiastes

"And moreover I saw under the sun the place of judgment, that wickedness was there; and the place of righteousness, that iniquity was there. I said in mine heart, God shall judge the righteous and the wicked: for there is a time there for every purpose and for every work." (3:16,17)

"For he that is higher than the highest regardeth." (5:8)

"Whoso keepeth the commandment shall feel no evil thing: and a wise man's heart discerneth both time and judgment. Because to every purpose there is time and judgment." (8:5,6)

"Rejoice, O young man, in thy youth; and let thy heart cheer thee in the days of thy youth, and walk in the ways of thine heart, and in the sight of thine eyes: but know thou, that for all these things God will bring thee into judgment." (11:9)

9

"For God shall bring every work into judgment, with every secret thing, whether it be good, or whether it be evil." (12:14)

The Safety of the Ark

There was a wonderful refuge in the Ark. God who had told Noah to come in and had shut the door, saved him by water. "When these things begin to come to pass, then look up, and lift up your heads; for your redemption draweth nigh." When the first rains came, Noah was just a solar year away from the New World.

There was no safety outside the Ark. So it is now as we look at the bread and wine. Here is safety – the God-provided atonement, pitched within and without.

The Ark came to rest on Mount Ararat on the same day of the same month as the Lord Jesus Christ was raised from the dead. There is a divinely provided type here, especially since Ararat means 'creation', 'holy land'. And so it will be for all of us who enter and remain in the Ark: we shall arrive at the new creation and the holiness of life in the kingdom of God.

3

PREPARING FOR HIS COMING
22nd January

Genesis 37   Psalms 39,40   **Matthew 24**

THE Olivet Prophecy is the most extensive explanation of prophecy made by the Lord Jesus Christ before the book of Revelation was given to John. It is to be found in three of the four Gospels: Matthew, Mark and Luke. The circumstances, as recorded by Matthew, which gave rise to the prophecy are interesting in themselves. The Lord had pronounced the doom of God's house (Matthew 23:38) and had said that they would not see him again until they proclaimed, "Blessed is he that cometh in the name of the Lord". That time has not yet arrived.

Jesus walked out of the temple with the disciples who drew his attention to the remarkable buildings of the temple complex. Jesus responded in a totally different vein: "Amen, I say unto you, There shall not be left here one stone upon another, that shall not be thrown down." This was a devastating pronouncement – even more devastating than the disciples realised, though they understood he was referring to the destruction of the temple. What they did not realise at the time was that if the temple was to be destroyed, then the whole Mosaic system of sacrifice would come to an end.

Tell us more

The group descended into the valley of the Kidron, crossed over and climbed the hill on the other side where they sat down. This was the Mount of Olives, and the temple, one of the then wonders of the world, shone in all its splendour over against them. But the Lord God was forsaking His house and would soon rend in two the veil of the temple. In another forty years the temple would be on fire and would be razed to the ground. Later still, in the reign of the emperor Hadrian, Zion was ploughed as a field as foretold by Micah the prophet.

11

But the doom of Zion brought no joy to Jesus. The Spirit's record through Luke tells us that as the Lord spoke of Jerusalem's fate he wept (19:41). She had missed the time of her visitation and had rejected her Man of Peace. We should take note in our own age and not "rejoice in calamities" which is denounced in Proverbs 17:5.

The disciples were stimulated by the words of Jesus and asked three questions:

"Tell us, when shall these things be?"

"What shall be the sign of thy coming?"

"And of the end of the world (age)?"

These three questions the Lord proceeds to answer and goes well beyond the disciples' first thoughts. He deals with two principal events, interweaving his words concerning them as if he is describing a single event, even though they were to be separated by at least 1,900 years. He spoke of the fall of Jerusalem to the Romans and of the time when the city would be revived in readiness for the day when she would say: "Blessed is he that cometh in the name of the Lord."

The answers that the Lord Jesus gave were not simply expositions of prophecy; they were designed to prepare the disciples for the dramatic events which would sweep over them. All of the stable things of life would be shaken, even the new things in Christ. To have been left in ignorance could have devastated the faith of many disciples.

The Signs

First, the Lord warned them to watch out for various signs.

- There would be false Christs, false prophets with great signs and wonders (Matthew 24:4,5,24,25) which would be very powerful.
- There would be wars and rumours of wars, strife amongst kingdoms, famines and earthquakes.
- The Gospel would be preached throughout the world.
- The "abomination of desolation" would stand up.
- The disciples would have to flee.

We know from scripture that some of these things happened before the fall of Jerusalem. The Acts of the

12

Apostles records false Christs, famines, and tension amongst kingdoms. Most of the New Testament books were written before Jerusalem fell and therefore do not record that event.

Profane historians record several famines, including two in Rome; there are records of earthquakes, including one in Jerusalem mentioned by Josephus, one in Rome, one in Crete and others.

But the words of Jesus make at least three references to Old Testament scriptures. How to deal with false prophets and their signs and wonders is dealt with in Deuteronomy 13; the "abomination of desolation" (Matthew 24:15) is a reference to Daniel 9:27 etc., and Jesus said, "Whoso readeth, let him understand"; and the eagle is referred to in Deuteronomy 28:49. Luke's record reads: "When ye shall see Jerusalem compassed with armies, then know that the desolation thereof is nigh." In other words, Christ is holding hands with Moses and the prophets.

The amazing flight of the disciples from the besieged city of Jerusalem is recorded in profane and religious history. On two occasions during the siege it was possible to flee from the Roman soldiers with the eagle as their emblem. Eusebius records that the disciples who fled went to Pella in Perea.

It requires little imagination to see the parallels between the fall of Judaea and the end of our age. The Lord's language is clearly designed to alert us to the perils of our own time and to prepare us for his coming. We have to flee from Babylon the Great before its fall – the apostate churches of Christendom and all of the associated heresies and ways of life. We too have had great warnings of one kind and another that should stimulate us to review our lives and prepare for the Day of the Lord.

Those who did not flee from Jerusalem were caught in one of the most horrible desolations in history. Even the less florid accounts make it plain that hundreds of thousands perished in the siege, and thousands more were taken captive.

The Second Coming

It is interesting to decide where in Matthew's record of the Olivet prophecy we pass from the events of the fall of Jerusalem to the events leading to the Second Coming. For example, is verse 29 about our own age? It is possible to say that the events described in this verse are a brief synopsis of the sixth seal in the book of Revelation (6:12-17). Jesus could not say more at this time because he had not yet received the Apocalypse from his Father: that did not occur until after he had gone to heaven.

On the other hand, Brother Thomas regarded the verse as a description of the collapse of the Jewish nation when their rulers, civil and religious, fell from their places of eminence and ceased to exist as the 'heavens'.

The fact is that the end of the Jewish world during the first century AD is intended to be a parallel of the end of our own age. The downfall of Jerusalem was a visitation of the Roman armies under the direction of the Lord Jesus Christ. It was a day of the Lord, a "coming" of Jesus, perhaps the coming described in the words, "Ye shall not have gone over the cities of Israel, till the Son of man be come".

But the great sound of a trumpet in verse 31 ties in with a number of powerful scriptures, notably the seventh trumpet of the book of Revelation, the descent of the Lord from heaven with the sound of a trumpet, and the resurrection described by Paul as a time when "the trumpet shall sound, and the dead shall be raised incorruptible, and we shall be changed". All these passages are based on the two silver trumpets of the priests in the tabernacle which were used for the warning and assembly of the Jewish people. When the trumpet sounds we shall be gathered to the Lord Jesus Christ. It will be a time even more dramatic and more decisive for each of us than the fall of Jerusalem was for that age.

The Lord's warnings to us

As we move through the chapter we are left in no doubt that the second event is being described. The disciples had asked for signs. They were given them, both for their own day and for ours. Our signs are beyond doubt:

1. *The sign of the fig tree putting forth its leaves.* The fig tree was one of three trees used to represent Israel in the prophets and by the Lord himself in his parable of the unfruitful fig tree (Luke 13:6 et seq.). The other trees were the olive and the vine. The Lord had blasted the fig tree in the last week of his earthly life because Judah was about to be withered as a nation by the disaster of the Roman overthrow. But there is hope of a tree if it be cut down leaving the roots intact. Israel was to put forth her leaves again. We – all of us, together and individually – are witnesses of these things.

But there is more. The record in Luke of the Olivet prophecy asks us to look at the fig tree and *all* the trees. Not only would the nation of Israel re-emerge but there would be an abundance of other trees shooting forth their leaves. Nationalism would become a sign of the times. Since the last war scores upon scores of new nations have emerged and found their places amongst the United Nations.

This process was accelerated by the breakdown of the old British Empire and the appearance of Third World and Arab countries. It goes further as witnessed by the unrest within the former Soviet territories and the national pressures within the Baltic states. Even in Britain there have been cries from Celtic and other ethnic groups.

All of us know well enough the words, "Verily I say unto you, This generation shall not pass, till all these things be fulfilled". In Christ's day these words brought about the downfall of Jerusalem in about forty years.

Whether forty years is the marker or not (and from what date) is not the main thrust of the warning. We are being told that the coming of the Lord is within a humanly measurable and understandable time of the resurrection of the Israelite nation and the emergence of other nations likewise. We have been warned.

2. *The sign from Noah's day.* Sometimes this is read as though merely normal life would be going on – eating, drinking, marrying and giving in marriage. It was not like that in Noah's day. The marriages were not normal. Genesis 6 reads: "They took them wives of all that they

chose". They married not according to God's choice but their own. The consequences were disastrous.

We do not have to look far for this sign in our own age. Marrying and giving in marriage has all kinds of connotations in our age. Only fourteen per cent of the population, according to a recent poll, thinks that cohabitation instead of marriage is wrong.

We can be sure too that the eating and drinking of Noah's day were abnormal. They were probably excessive and greatly self-indulgent, and this marked them out as forgetful of God.

It cannot be a coincidence that the Lord's parable at the end of Matthew 24 concerns the servant who says that his lord delays his coming. Whether he did this in words and by conscious decision or by his behaviour matters not in this context. That was how he dealt with life. Notice the consequence: he began to eat and drink with the drunken.

Signs from without affect the ecclesia within and we need to take stock of ourselves and our families.

3. *Men's hearts failing them for fear*, and for looking after those things which are coming upon the world constitute another prominent sign according to the account in Luke. Our complex way of living leaves us wide open to all kinds of disasters, troubles and unrest. Man has poisoned his morals by his self-indulgence; he has poisoned the world in which he lives by his greed and lack of care. If no other evils were performed, enough has been done already to the relationships among people and the very earth and atmosphere on which we depend to make it certain that many more disasters of one kind or another will overtake us. We have been warned.

The Remedy

We are not able to work out the exact time of the Lord's coming. Jesus told us we would not: "Therefore be ye also ready: for in such an hour as ye think not the Son of man cometh." Therefore the remedy does not lie in pinpointing the time of the Lord's return but in being ready whenever he comes – "and so much the more as ye see the day approaching".

The word for household in Matthew 24:45 is most interesting. It has two meanings: 'household' and 'healing'. For example, in Revelation 22:2 it occurs in the phrase, "the leaves of the tree were for the *healing* of the nations". The household is a place of healing. It is here – centred on the Lord's table and the emblems that remind us of his love – that we shall find the remedies for our spiritual ills, both known and unknown. We must resolve to make maximum use of our opportunities.

The ecclesia needs you and you need the ecclesia – it is the body of Christ. How we treat it is how we treat Christ. Let us resolve to put our efforts into making the greatest contribution we can. It is more important than our eating and drinking, than our marrying and giving in marriage – it is for our lives.

17

COMFORT OF THE SCRIPTURES

4

VESSELS

Exodus 3,4   Psalms 56,57   **Romans 9**

IN the New Testament reading for today we read of vessels of various kinds. They are marked out particularly in Romans 9 as "vessels of wrath" and "vessels of mercy". The former are fitted for destruction, and the latter for glory. Vessels are receptacles or containers for fluids or solids. Their size varies from the blood vessels of the body to the enormous supertankers on the high seas. A spoon, cup, plate, jug, vase, pan and a thousand and one other utensils come to mind when we read the word.

In the Bible the idea is used figuratively as well as in its literal sense. We learn that Paul was a chosen vessel (Acts 9:15); and in today's readings we meet a number of people whose destinies are totally different even though each of them is a vessel himself.

You and I are vessels, and need to answer some searching questions. What are we being used for, and who is using us? How much do we contain? Is there room for more? Are we filling up the measures of our fathers, as Jesus described the evil generation of his day, or are we being reserved for a greater use in the temple of the Lord?

Let us pursue a path in the word of God and take lessons and take heart as we go along together.

Ezra and his Companions

Ezra undertakes the journey from Babylon to Jerusalem in wondrous faith and in prayer. He prepared his heart to seek God and His law, and we can see in his comments that he was aware of two kinds of vessels: vessels of mercy and vessels of wrath: "The hand of our God is upon all them for good that seek him; but his power and his wrath is against all them that forsake him" (Ezra 8:22).

In preparation for the perilous journey to Jerusalem, Ezra commits to the priests special charges of gold, silver and vessels (verse 25), and with them this special word of warning:

"Ye are holy unto the LORD; the vessels are holy also; and the silver and the gold are a freewill offering unto the LORD God of your fathers. Watch ye, and keep them, until ye weigh them before the chief of the priests and the Levites, and chief of the fathers of Israel, at Jerusalem, in the chambers of the house of the LORD."

(verses 28,29)

The priests were holy and their vessels were holy. The obvious parallel between them and us as chosen of the Lord is clear for all to see. We are on the way to Jerusalem from Babylon and our vessels – our lives – are for use in the kingdom. One day we shall give account before the Chief of the Priests. Then we shall be weighed; let us not be found wanting.

We have taken a charge from the Lord Jesus Christ and we must fulfil that which we have promised. Our vessels are not ours but his. Let us remember the charge and take hold of ourselves in faith and love.

What Size?

One of our failings is that we are always comparing ourselves with other people, for better or for worse. Some of us get discouraged because we are not as capable in our own estimation as others who seem able to do more or better than we can. There is a message in the Bible references to vessels that provides an answer to concerns like these.

In any house there are many sizes of vessel from the glass dropper for placing drops in the eyes, to the tanks for water. Buckets, spoons, jugs, cups, and containers of all other kinds and sizes are available to us. All have their uses. The bucket is no good for dispensing eye drops, and the spoon is no use for putting water on a blazing fire. Each must be suitable to its task, and it is no different in the spiritual sphere. The important thing for us is to be of use to the capacity of which we are capable in the Lord's service. The Lord has called us: he wants to use us now and in eternity. We have been called, if we remain true to our calling, to be vessels of mercy.

Remember the widow woman in Elisha's time. Every vessel, wherever it came from, was filled with oil when it came into the house of blessing and of wonder. None was empty except those which were not brought for service. Again, there is a lesson for us. The Lord will never leave us without work to do for him. Most of the work is unspectacular, but it may nevertheless be powerful – like prayer and faith.

Moreover, the former uses to which we put our vessel are not a barrier to holy service. One of the most comforting aspects of the Exodus account reminds us that things brought by the children of Israel from Egypt went into the tabernacle service. And Peter's nets that had plied his trade before he ever heard of the Lord Jesus were used for a miraculous draught of fishes.

But if our vessel is full of our own things – self-concern, pleasure, indulgence, sin – there will be little room for the things of the Lord. The secret of life is to empty one's self of other things. The account of the shipwreck in Acts 27 provides a stark warning about the presence of unnecessary cargo. The sailors jettisoned a great deal from the vessel in which Paul was sailing to Rome when the life of those on board was in danger. So it is with us. Have a look at your cargo.

Today, commercial shipping is required to register what it carries. The list of its cargo is included on the ship's manifest – a document giving comprehensive details of the contents, cargo, passengers and crew. When the Lord examines your life and mine, what will he think of the ship's manifest? Are we laden with too many of this world's goods, and at risk of being swamped by the storms of life?

Remember the words concerning the Lord Jesus Christ: "He made himself of no reputation" ("he emptied himself", RV) (Philippians 2.7). This can only mean that he carried no unnecessary cargo. But was he really empty? For when the Lord God his Father looked upon him, he was "full of grace and truth" (John 1:14). The Lord's example shows us that godly vessels carry godly cargo.

Are we predestined to mercy or to wrath?

This is one of the deep questions of scripture. Sometimes people get very disheartened because they think that they are one of the failures, one of the vessels of wrath and that there is little they can do about it. It is useful to get things straight, whatever difficulties we may have with predestination and foreknowledge, which are God's prerogative anyway.

1. If God has called us, He has not called us to be a vessel of wrath. His calling is one of mercy.

2. Nobody who truly wants to be in the kingdom of God will be excluded because God has predestined him or her to destruction. What we truly want, what we truly believe and strive for, we shall get.

3. None of us is perfect. All of us are sinners called to be saints. We are vessels of mercy not vessels of perfect works.

4. Having been called, our destiny is now in our own hands. We can work out our way as though we had never been called; or we can devote ourselves to God and the Lord Jesus Christ.

Examine the teaching of Jeremiah 18:1-10 about the divine potter. The vessels were formed according to the way they reacted to the potter. So it is with us in our day; none of us is predestined to destruction, but we may end there if we choose not to respond wisely and well to the calling we have received.

We have this treasure

We need to recognize the fact that it is not the vessel but its contents and its use which are holy. There were ornate vessels used in the service of idols; they looked good, and were often made of the most precious materials, but they were abhorrent to God. They were priceless vessels of silver and gold which never in their service rose above satisfying the wishes of dissolute people in their feasting and godlessness. For us it is different:

"We have this treasure in earthen vessels, that the excellency of the power may be of God, and not of us."

(2 Corinthians 4:7)

The barrel of meal that was never empty was an earthen vessel. But the miracle was not about the barrel; the miracle happened inside. The pitcher which Gideon used, and his men likewise, was an earthen vessel, but the victory over the Midianites did not come from the Israelites' vessels – it came from the light which they contained and the trumpet which announced the work of the Lord.

The wonder of God's word and purpose is happening within us, within this mortal frame; inside is the inner man, the new man in Christ Jesus. It is the light that will shine in glory in the day of Christ when the trumpet shall sound and the dead shall be raised.

But the lesson is one of humility: "What hast thou that thou didst not receive?" (1 Corinthians 4:7). The glory is the Lord's.

Be ye clean

It is difficult to remain clean when travelling a road which is filthy. It is impossible to isolate ourselves from the world in which we live, nevertheless we are called to be clean:

"Depart ye, depart ye, go ye out from thence, touch no unclean thing; go ye out of the midst of her; be ye clean, that bear the vessels of the LORD."   (Isaiah 52:11)

The call is clear: we must flee Babylon and the Babylonish garment. There are ways of life in Babylon which must not be carried over into the house of the Lord.

"Nevertheless the foundation of God standeth sure, having this seal, The Lord knoweth them that are his. And, Let every one that nameth the name of Christ depart from iniquity. But in a great house there are not only vessels of gold and of silver, but also of wood and of earth; and some to honour, and some to dishonour. If a man therefore purge himself from these, he shall be a vessel unto honour, sanctified, and meet for the master's use, and prepared unto every good work."

(2 Timothy 2:19-21)

Yes, the Lord knows those who are His and shows them compassion:

23

"Thou tellest my wanderings: put thou my tears into thy bottle: are they not in thy book?"

(Psalm 56:8)

Weighed before the Lord

Ezra's priests were to appear before the chief of the priests and the vessels carried by them were to be weighed. We too will stand before the Chief Priest and our vessels will be weighed. Let us remember Belshazzar who used the vessels in his possession wrongly, and was weighed in the balances and found wanting. Let us recall the foolish virgins – for they too had vessels and knew where to find oil, but they failed to be ready for the great moment and were empty when they should have been full.

As we meet to remember the Lord, may we have oil in our lamps; may our vessels be consecrated to the Master's use, that when he comes we might be told that he has use for us as vessels of honour – the final stage for all vessels of mercy.

"Blessed are the merciful: for they shall obtain mercy."   (Matthew 5:7)

5

THE VICTORY OF THE KING
19th February

Exodus 30 **Psalms 87,88** **Mark 15,16**

IN the first Old Testament reading (Exodus 30) we have an account of the little golden altar which stood before the veil and on which was offered incense by the High Priest every morning and every evening. There is too a description of the holy anointing oil which contained myrrh and was used to anoint all the vessels for service and the priests, and of the incense which was myrrh free, a portion of which was kept in the most holy place before the Lord.

These spoke of Christ and his mighty work of redemption accomplished by the word of God and prayer, and sanctified by the sweet incense of praise.

Psalm 88 speaks of a man of great suffering and loneliness, rejected and separated from friends and acquaintances. In this is portrayed the Lord Jesus Christ in his desolation and yet, in his prayers daily, and in the morning like the little golden altar he calls upon the God of his salvation (verse 1).

The Reality in Christ

But it is in the Gospels that the awful truth is recounted. All the types and shadows give place to the heavenly tabernacle which is Christ whom the Lord pitched and not man. Everything, every colour, every part, every sacrifice and motion, every feast and remembrance were brought together in him.

He who is King was first to be crowned with thorns before the Crown of Glory was his. Whilst he suffered, all the types and shadows would be seen and all the prophets would stand around in their words in testimony that he was the Word made flesh.

Pilate, the puppet of Caesar, had no purpose except to save his own skin; no overriding sense of justice with which to withstand the wicked and devious machinations

25

of the elders of the Jews. Even so the word of God, unknown to him, was fulfilled before his eyes and in his hearing.

"And the chief priests accused him of many things: but he answered nothing. And Pilate asked him again, saying, Answerest thou nothing? behold how many things they witness against thee." (Mark 15:3,4)

But Isaiah was very near and the Spirit's words silenced his Lord's tongue:

"He was oppressed, and he was afflicted, yet he opened not his mouth: he is brought as a lamb to the slaughter, and as a sheep before her shearers is dumb, so he openeth not his mouth." (Isaiah 53:7)

The two Sons

Amongst the most despicable deeds of the rulers and the people was the choice of Barabbas instead of Christ. Every sense of right and of justice was grievously violated. Even so, the choice was such as to illumine Christ. Barabbas means 'son of a father' but Christ was the only begotten Son of the Father. The one was a murderer – a life taker – and the other the *giver* of life eternal.

The Scourging

Barabbas was released but Jesus was taken to be scourged before being delivered to be crucified. The barbaric cruelty of this is unbelievable. It was done merely to please the people and not for any evil that Christ had done. The act was screaming out for retribution and judgement upon the perpetrator(s). There was no word from Christ. "Is it lawful to scourge a man that is ... uncondemned?" was Paul's justified defence. But now there was an ancient word which held everything in check:

"The Lord GOD hath opened mine ear, and I was not rebellious, neither turned away back. I gave my back to the smiters, and my cheeks to them that plucked off the hair: I hid not my face from shame and spitting ... Behold, the Lord GOD will help me; who is he that shall condemn me?" (Isaiah 50:5,6,9)

The Palace of Sin

The Praetorium (palace) was the next scene of defamation. The whole cohort of soldiers played the game of king with the King, and crowned him with thorns – "thorns also and thistles shall it bring forth to thee" – and they mocked his true title, The King of the Jews. But their colours paid silent testimony to the Law – red-purple with his fine twined linen. And it shall come to pass that every knee shall bow. Every soldier the world over will kneel as will every ruler and every common man. It will all come to pass; not a word from God will fall to the ground.

Led

Jesus willingly went to Calvary. His adversaries would have had no power if that were not the case. All four Gospels use the same word: Christ was "led" – not driven, dragged or forced. He was:

"As a lamb that is led to the slaughter."

(Isaiah 53:7, RV)

The Gospel Call

Simon the Cyrenian was impressed to be ready to help with the cross. Like his namesake the Pharisee, who was addressed by Christ with "I have somewhat to say unto thee" (Luke 7:40), the man from Cyrene had much to learn. He saw more and saw it more closely than any others. Right from the city wall to Golgotha he learned of Christ. There was no blasphemy or threatening behaviour, no unseemly speech, no self-pity; only a wondrous bearing of his wretchedness and ignominy. A nobleman indeed. This father of Alexander and Rufus must assuredly have told the tale to his family. Did they respond to the Gospel? Else, why would the Gospel name them? And is the Rufus and his mother of Romans 16:13 this very man?

Golgotha

Golgotha means 'the place of a skull'. Perhaps it looked like that. Perhaps it had other significance. For this was the place where Goliath's skull was buried when David brought it to Zion so long ago. The slaying of the giant is given much more meaning in the Psalms. When there was no chance of human victory, God provided the way that the son of man might have victory over the enemy and the avenger (Psalm 8:2). "Mine enemies … shall fall and perish at thy presence" (Psalm 9:3). There it was in

27

Golgotha that the giant sin was finally smitten by the stone which the builders rejected.

The Greatest Temptation?

The taunts of wicked men must have brought the greatest temptation to mind: "If thou be the Son of God, come down from the cross"; from the malefactor: "If thou be Christ, save thyself". Twelve legions of angels were at his behest. We must thank God that our Lord surrendered himself to save us, and in so doing he *did* save himself.

His Garments

His earthly possessions became the perquisites of the four soldiers. But even they had a quandary – the seamless robe. It was too good to spoil; it had to remain intact. It was like the robe of a priest in its meaning. It was like the wholeness of the character of Christ in which his manhood and divine Sonship were blended without seam. It represented his perfect righteousness.

"Hear, O heavens, and give ear, O earth"

All creation was to pay its homage. The sun hid its face as though in shame and there was darkness, as over Egypt, before the death of the firstborn. The darkness was at least over all the land of Israel, if not even more widely. What did Caesar think? And the elders and chief priests?

The earth trembled as at Sinai – a witness of things yet to come when the Lord shall yet once more shake, not the earth only, but also heaven and the sea, and the dry land.

And then there is the inexpressible meaning of "My God, my God, why hast thou forsaken me?" (Psalm 22:1). Maybe Jesus spoke these words aloud as he commenced to recite to himself the whole of the Psalm.

The Reed

In his dying moments there was a further witness from the Law. Christ needed moisture for his mouth in order to speak his last words. The sponge filled with vinegar was passed up to him on a hyssop reed. Hyssop was used at Passover, when the first covenant was given, for the cleansing of the leper, for the wonderful work of cleansing from death in the red heifer, and at the day of atonement. It had to be a hyssop reed at Calvary to fulfil all the types.

28

Final Words

Mark says he cried with a loud voice. We know what he said: "It is finished" – words so like the end of Psalm 22 – and, "Father, into thy hands I commend my spirit" (John 19:30; Luke 23:46). The word was made flesh in the double sense – by birth and by living and dying. Everything had been perfected.

His Dying

No one records simply, "He died". Mark and John say, he "gave up the spirit"; Matthew, "He yielded up his spirit" (27:50, RV); and Luke, "Into thy hands I commend my spirit: and having said thus, he gave up the spirit" (23:46). It is almost as though there was a conscious surrendering of the last breath, the rendering back of that originally given when God "breathed into his nostrils the breath of life".

The Temple

At that moment the great veil in the temple was rent by an invisible hand from top to bottom – an act of God that the way into the holiest might be made known. In the absence of all others this declaration came from the mouth of a nameless Gentile: "Truly this man was the Son of God". He glorified God, saying, "Certainly this was a righteous man".

The other Joseph

There was a Joseph at his birth. There was a Joseph at his death, of honourable estate, coming with myrrh and aloes along with his friend Nicodemus, who at last came out into the open. Now barred from keeping the Passover, they gave the Passover Lamb a good if hasty burial. Christ was "with the rich in his death" (Isaiah 53:9).

The Tomb

"Wherein was never man yet laid": here was a deeper truth than ever man perceived. There had never been a tomb in which a perfectly righteous man had lain. The great stone at the door was no barrier when the time arrived. When the sun was risen all was made known. The angel sitting on the stone signified that the great work was over. "A young man sitting on the right side" was itself a witness of things to come when after the ascension it would be wonderfully true that in the presence of the Father there is "a young man sitting on the right side".

All these details are present in the simple emblems on the Lord's table, and they show forth his death, until he come.

6

THE POWER OF GOD
20th February

Exodus 31,32   Psalm 89   **1 Corinthians 1,2**

THERE are times when the power of God is made manifest in dramatic acts which dwarf mere man – the crossing of the Red Sea, the feeding of the 5,000, the stilling of the storm on Galilee, for example. We tend to think of the power of God as the manifestation, for want of a better word, of powerful physical phenomena.

Indeed, in everyday life we think of power in terms of what can be done by it – horsepower, electric power, manpower and the like. It is interesting that when God reveals Himself He does not speak in those terms:

"And the LORD passed by before him, and proclaimed, The LORD, The LORD God, merciful and gracious, long-suffering, and abundant in goodness and truth, keeping mercy for thousands, forgiving iniquity and transgression and sin, and that will by no means clear the guilty; visiting the iniquity of the fathers upon the children, and upon the children's children, unto the third and to the fourth generation."   (Exodus 34:6,7)

Why?

Why is the physical power not in this manifestation of God's glory? It must be because it is not part of His name. It is a spiritual matter because God is a spiritual being. Moreover that is the important thing for us to know. Even so, when Moses learned of the name, he thought in terms of power; not physical power, but something far greater, the very essence of redemption.

When Israel sinned grievously in murmuring against God and expressing a longing to return to Egypt, God said:

"I will smite them with the pestilence, and disinherit them, and will make of thee a greater nation and mightier than they."   (Numbers 14:12)

Once more Moses stood in the breach and for the nation:

31

"And now, I beseech thee, let the power of my Lord be great, according as thou hast spoken, saying, The LORD is longsuffering, and of great mercy, forgiving iniquity and transgression, and by no means clearing the guilty, visiting the iniquity of the fathers upon the children unto the third and fourth generation."

(verses 17,18)

Forgiveness is the great power of God; that is how Moses understood it. Perhaps in our prayers or even at baptismal services we do not regard forgiveness as calling for the power of God. Moses tells us that forgiveness does not call for the power of God, it *is* the great power of God.

Illustration

Amidst all the surrounding people, and much to the consternation of the Pharisees who were present, Jesus forgave sins:

"And when he saw their faith, he said unto him, Man, thy sins are forgiven thee." (Luke 5:20)

There were murmurings and thoughts in their hearts that this was blasphemy since God alone can forgive sins. No one among such people perceived that Christ was God made manifest on earth and therefore *authorised* (the other word for power) on God's behalf to forgive sins. This concept was beyond them though they often asked for a sign in proof of Jesus' authority. Without waiting and in direct answer to their thoughts the Lord said:

"What reason ye in your hearts? Whether is easier, to say, Thy sins be forgiven thee; or to say, Rise up and walk? But that ye may know that the Son of man hath power upon earth to forgive sins (he said unto the sick of the palsy), I say unto thee, Arise, and take up thy couch, and go into thine house." (verses 22-24)

For him the two things were part of the same process, a process which is described for us in a preceding verse:

"And it came to pass on a certain day, as he was teaching, that there were Pharisees and doctors of the law sitting by, which were come out of every town of Galilee, and Judæa, and Jerusalem: and the power of the Lord was present to heal them." (verse 17)

32

The power to heal was primarily spiritual healing of which the physical healing was an evidence. The scriptures had often made this link:

"The Spirit of the Lord GOD is upon me; because the LORD hath anointed me to preach good tidings unto the meek; he hath sent me to bind up the brokenhearted, to proclaim liberty to the captives, and the opening of the prison to them that are bound; to proclaim the acceptable year of the LORD, and the day of vengeance of our God; to comfort all that mourn." (Isaiah 61:1,2)

"Bless the LORD, O my soul, and forget not all his benefits: who forgiveth all thine iniquities; who healeth all thy diseases." (Psalms 103:2,3)

The Root

The thought is simple and the reason for this is simple. It was sin – the spiritual evil – which brought disease and death into the world. Therefore the remedy must be first the forgiving of our sins and then the healing of all our diseases in the day to come.

The remedy in Christ is declared of God:

"But unto them which are called, both Jews and Greeks, Christ the power of God, and the wisdom of God." (1 Corinthians 1:24)

"That no flesh should glory in his presence. But of him are ye in Christ Jesus, who of God is made unto us wisdom, and righteousness, and sanctification, and redemption." (verse 29,30)

"That your faith should not stand in the wisdom of men, but in the power of God." (2:5)

The Power in us

It has been a subject for discussion from time to time as to what is meant by the Holy Spirit, of which our bodies are a temple: "Know ye not that ye are the temple of God, and that the Spirit of God dwelleth in you?" (1 Corinthians 3:16). Some have seen it simply as God's power implanted in us and of course others have linked this with spirit gifts and other things. It is perhaps easier and helps to clear away the mist surrounding these things when we recognise the Spirit's description of where we were before we came into the Truth:

"To open their eyes, and to turn them from darkness to light, and from the power of Satan unto God, that they may receive forgiveness of sins, and inheritance among them which are sanctified by faith that is in me."
(Acts 26:18)

That which works in us is from God:

"Now we have received, not the spirit of the world, but the spirit which is of God; that we might know the things that are freely given to us of God."
(1 Corinthians 2:12)

"For who hath known the mind of the Lord, that he may instruct him? But we have the mind of Christ."
(verse 16)

This mind of Christ is the mind of the Spirit. It is divine thinking begotten by faith in the word of God which liveth and abideth for ever. The mind of the Lord is the Spirit of the Lord as will be seen from the following quotations in which the second is the New Testament version of the first:

"Who hath directed the Spirit of the LORD, or being his counsellor hath taught him?" (Isaiah 40:13)

"For who hath known the mind of the Lord? or who hath been his counsellor?" (Romans 11:34)

Summing up these things we have plain testimony:

"For I am not ashamed of the gospel of Christ: for it is the power of God unto salvation to every one that believeth; to the Jew first, and also to the Greek."
(Romans 1:16)

"For the preaching of the cross is to them that perish foolishness; but unto us which are saved it is the power of God." (1 Corinthians 1:18)

"And what is the exceeding greatness of his power to us-ward who believe, according to the working of his mighty power, which he wrought in Christ, when he raised him from the dead, and set him at his own right hand in the heavenly places, far above all principality, and power, and might, and dominion, and every name that is named, not only in this world, but also in that which is to come." (Ephesians 1:19-21)

Application

It becomes clear that each of us has a power within which stems from the word of Christ dwelling in us richly. This power we exercise in our daily fight against sin and in our preaching of the word of God.

But there is an aspect of this that we greatly underrate. There is power in our relationships one with another; for example, we have within our grasp the power of forgiveness, forgiveness of others. Peter imagined that he was being magnanimous were he to find it in his heart to forgive his offending brother seven times. But he missed the point. Forgiveness is a power that is inexhaustible. We shall need it to the end of our days because of our own personal sins. But the power of God's forgiveness is limited by our willingness to forgive each other.

If we truly believe in the forgiveness of God, then we must allow that power to move us to the salvation of others by forgiving them. Otherwise we restrict our own salvation. The parable of the 10,000 talents is surely the evidence here.

This is a power to be released in our ecclesias, in our homes, in our marriages, in our dealings with those outside. Forgiveness is powerful to cleanse and to energize us in our daily living. It expels bitterness and hate, acrimony and offence.

"Death and life are in the power of the tongue: and they that love it shall eat the fruit thereof."

(Proverbs 18:21)

"(God) hath delivered us from the power of darkness, and hath translated us into the kingdom of his dear Son." (Colossians 1:13)

The power of God is revealed most wonderfully in the Lord's sacrifice. Our remembrance of it can be powerful too, if we are humbled and prepare ourselves once again to learn its great lessons.

7

THE RIGHT HAND
4th March

Leviticus 9,10   **Psalms 108,109**   2 Corinthians 1,2

THERE can be no doubt from our recent readings and our readings today that emphasis is placed in scripture on the right hand. Whether it is the right hand of a person or object, or someone standing or sitting at someone else's right hand, there is always a great importance attached to it.

The emphasis is not confined to persons; it extends also to animals under the law and to arrangements in the tabernacle and the temple.

It is clear that we are intended to take lessons from what we read, and these are not too far to seek.

The Place

The East is on the right hand side as one faces north, and this is how it is described in scripture. Thus the tribe of Judah was the standard bearer on the east side of the encampment (Numbers 2:3) and that standard corresponds to the face of the lion in the vision of Ezekiel 1 and is on the right side (Ezekiel 1:10).

Thus the place of the sun's rising, the east, is the place of the Lion of the Tribe of Judah. There is a fittingness about that. Christ is the Lion of the tribe of Judah and he is the sun that will rise and shine upon the earth. Furthermore, in Ezekiel's vision (43:1,2), the glory returns by the way of the east and comes to the house of God.

There is similar evidence that the east is the right hand in the record of the boundaries of the tribes. For example:

"And the coast of Manasseh was ... before Shechem; and the border went along on the right hand unto the inhabitants of En-Tappuah (which lay to the east of Shechem)."   (Joshua 17:7)

This should not surprise us because the cherubim were placed at the east of the garden of Eden. Nevertheless, worship in the tabernacle was not directed *towards* the east as in sun worship, but with one's back to the east. In other words one stood, as it were, in the place of the right hand and looked outwards to the west.

In our daily lives we need to be correctly orientated; that is, our life must be governed and take its own bearings from the east, the Son of Righteousness, the son of the right hand. It is all too easy to take one's daily bearings from other things – our work, our family, our desires, our leisure, our money. This will be disastrous in the end. Unless we have got our primary bearings right, we shall have everything wrong. Only in this way shall we be faithfully on the way to the kingdom of God. Our lives should always have Christ on the right hand side, the place of highest importance and the place from which everything else takes it direction.

Anatomically

Our right hand is normally our strongest and accordingly it has a significance in everyday speech – right-hand man, for example. This is true biblically as well. The firstborn is 'the man of my right hand'; he is the beginning of strength.

It is for this reason that Joseph received a double portion in Israel by having two tribes compared with everyone else's one tribe, and said Jacob, Joseph's was the birthright (1 Chronicles 5:2).

Once again the lessons are clear. We must have the right attitude to our Heavenly Father and His Son:

"I have set the LORD always before me: because he is at my right hand, I shall not be moved."   (Psalm 16:8)

"Thy right hand hath holden me up."   (Psalm 18:35)

"Thy right hand upholdeth me."   (Psalm 63:8)

"A wise man's heart is at his right hand; but a fool's heart at his left."   (Ecclesiastes 10:2)

If we are relying on some other right hand, some other source for our help, we shall fail miserably at the end. We need to ask the questions of ourselves urgently and without running away from the implications. Where does our reliance lie? What do we resort to first of all? What kind of hand guides our lives? We all know the real answer to those questions.

If God is not at our right hand then there is a comment in today's psalm which should be a warning for us:

"Let Satan stand at his right hand." (Psalm 109:6) This is the psalm that is about Judas and is so quoted by Peter in Acts 1:20. Therefore, it is also a Psalm about the Lord Jesus Christ who says:

"Help me, O LORD my God: O save me according to thy mercy: that they may know that this is thy hand; that thou, LORD, hast done it." (109:26,27)

This is developed even more beautifully in Psalm 73:

"Nevertheless I am continually with thee:
Thou hast holden me by my right hand.
Thou shalt guide me with thy counsel,
And afterward receive me to glory.
Whom have I in heaven but thee?
And there is none upon earth that I desire beside thee." (Psalm 73:23-25)

Examples under the Law

In our readings yesterday, we had the ritual and service of consecration of Aaron the high priest. In Leviticus 8:23,24 there was the ceremony of putting the blood of the ram of consecration upon the tip of Aaron's right ear, his right thumb and his right great toe.

These were three indicators of the work of the high priest. He had to listen to God and to the people; he had to do the work of the Lord and he had to walk in His court about His business. Therefore the right ear, thumb and great toe were marked with the blood.

We are the priesthood of the age to come and in some ways are the priesthood on probation (1 Peter 2:5). We have been consecrated by the blood of Christ. What do we do with our ears? Listen to gossip, to the poison of evil programmes on radio and TV? or to the word of God and the needs of our brethren and sisters and those outside who are seeking the light?

And our hands? What work do we do? Is the call of God the first call upon our strength and time and resources? What work have we done this week for Him?

And our feet? Where have they gone? Have they been amongst the beautiful feet that proclaim the Gospel of peace? Have they carried us in service to the sick, the afflicted, or to places of ill-repute and on missions that do disservice to God? Remember the High Priest of God and that we ourselves are consecrated to the Lord.

Under the law there were two portions of offerings given especially to the Lord and these were waved or lifted up before him. These were the wave breast, which does not concern us particularly at this time, and the other was the heave offering, the choice portion offered to the Lord which was given to the High Priest as the representative of God.

As explained in Numbers 18:18,19, the right shoulder (thigh or upper leg) was given in this way and lifted up before the Lord to extol and to praise Him. This was the strongest part of the body. The lesson is obvious and simple. All of our choicest strength is the Lord's. It must not be given to any one else or used for any other purpose. The brother who puts his major effort into his business and makes the Lord take second place has forgotten the heave offering. And how about those who put family before God? or summer cottages, or holidays, or friends of one kind and another? Brethren, these things ought not to be. It was from the peace offering and from the offerings of the firstborn that the heave offering was particularly taken. Only the best and not second best is good enough for God.

Sometimes we have to take drastic measures for the Lord:

"If thy right hand offend thee, cut it off, and cast it from thee: for it is profitable for thee that one of thy members should perish, and not that thy whole body should go into hell."   (Matthew 5:30, RV)

The Final Analysis

In the end, it is the right hand of the Lord that will determine our destiny, our eternal destiny. His hand is full of pleasures ("at thy right hand there are pleasures for evermore" – Psalm 16:11). Of wisdom it is said: "Length of days is in her right hand" (Proverbs 3:16).

"Save (us) with thy right hand" (Psalm 108:6) is the prayer contained in today's reading.

40

"Then shall the King say unto them on his right hand, Come, ye blessed of my Father, inherit the kingdom prepared for you from the foundation of the world." (Matthew 25:34)

As we prepare to partake of bread and wine, it is worth remembering that the judgement will be delivered by Jesus, who had a thief at his right hand in death and is now seated at the right hand of his Father in heaven.

8

COMING HOME
7th March

Leviticus 14   Psalms 115,116   2 Corinthians 8,9

IN the wilderness, there was a place called 'outside the camp', which was, of course, without the camp. It is hard for us to imagine what this meant. Those who were sent there, through no fault of their own, were outside the fellowship of the camp, cut off from their families.

For two of the groups who were outside the camp, the severance was for a comparatively short time: those who had been in contact with death and those who had an issue, for example.

There was however a group for whom being 'outside the camp' was like a death knell. These were the lepers. The disease caused them to lose parts of their body. In a sense it was a living death. Worst of all, there was no cure. Once the priest had diagnosed leprosy, the sufferer was cut off and there was no treatment; there was no therapy.

The exception

Although there was no human cure for the disease, there were occasions when the sufferer recovered from the disease and was restored whole. Since there was no human cure, healing could well have come from God.

Healthy though the former sufferer now was, he could not resume normal life in the camp without undergoing an elaborate divine ritual. Jesus spoke of this when he healed a leper by his touch and instructed him to show himself to the priest and offer the sacrifices commanded through Moses.

In various places in scripture, the language of leprosy is used: e.g. Psalms 38, 39, 51 and Isaiah 53. We know how appropriate this is when we consider that the wages of sin is death and acknowledge that there is no human cure. Salvation is by grace. This should destroy all human pride, for what have we that we did not receive?

The first day

The ritual was prescribed by the Lord to Moses (Leviticus 13,14). On the first day, the priest came outside the camp and examined the man carefully and then pronounced him free of the disease. There was a simple but intriguing ceremony. The former leper brings to the priest two clean living birds, perhaps sparrows, together with scarlet wool, cedar wood and hyssop which were used as the means of sprinkling the blood.

One of the birds was killed over an earthen vessel and over living water. This foreshadows our situation. All of us are earthen vessels, houses of clay as scripture tells us. We are cleansed by the water and the blood of Christ, and by the living water of the word of God.

The offerer was now sprinkled seven times by the blood collected in the earthen vessel. We remember the command to Naaman to wash in Jordan seven times and "be thou clean" – the very words used by Jesus when he healed the solitary leper – "I will, be thou clean". After the sevenfold sprinkling the priest now pronounced the man clean.

We must remember how we have been cleansed. It was by the very man whom the onlookers regarded as "smitten of God".

What of the other bird? It was taken with cedar wood, scarlet and hyssop, and dipped in the blood of the slain bird. Then, following the pronouncement that the leper was now clean, the second bird was loosed and let go free in the open field. We see death and freedom in the two birds, pointing forward to the death of Jesus our Lord and his resurrection when he was let go free, having broken the bonds of death.

The man now washed his body completely, and shaved off all his hair, everywhere, that he might be clean. All the outer places which may hitherto have been affected by the leprosy were now washed, ritually removing all his old life.

We, too, have to shed all our former way of life in sin and be clean.

Back into the camp

This 'resurrected' man now walked into the camp which he had never again expected to see. His family, friends and everyone else could see him. He was clean. Our hymns 29 and 30 ("After Thy loving kindness, Lord" and "Throughly wash me") are in fact the petitions of David in Psalm 51 cast into a prayer for us. Our cleansing must be a continuing process as we "cleanse ourselves from all filthiness of the flesh and spirit" (2 Corinthians 7:1) and seek to purify ourselves "even as he is pure" (1 John 3:3). But the man could not yet go home. He had to stay outside his house for seven days, openly to share his joy with everyone; passers by and children (who would doubtless ask questions as to why he was outside his house). "For this my son was dead, and is alive again; he was lost, and is found" (Luke 15:24). We should be proclaiming to all around us the saving work of the Lord, making known the peace which passeth all understanding.

Finally

On the seventh day the man washed his clothes, his whole body and once again removed all his hair. We, too, should shed our old habits and do this by resolution and prayer.

And now come greater wonders. As though it was not enough to be free of the dread disease and back in the camp of the Lord God, now the Lord gives abundant good measure, pressed down and running over. There is super-abundant joy and blessing. This is our God and let us never forget it.

It is the eighth day, the day when little baby boys (the leper's flesh is now like a little child's) entered the covenant. It was the day when the Lord Jesus Christ was raised.

The man brings a mixture of offerings and some oil. We need not trouble ourselves about all of the offerings but there are wonderful things to notice. Any Israelite would have caught his breath when he saw what was happening to the man who once had leprosy.

The priest put a little of the blood of one of the sacrifices on the tip of the man's right ear, on the thumb of his right hand and on the great toe of his right foot. Head, hand and foot – all of the man symbolically.

His eyes would open wide and, perhaps, tears ran from them. This very ritual was used when Aaron and his sons were consecrated in their office of priesthood! Sacred ears, sacred hands and sacred feet. Listening to God, working for Him and going forth on His work. We who are to be kings and priests should be similarly consecrated and not polluted by evil things.

But there was more to come. The priest poured oil into the palm of his left hand, dipped his right finger in the oil and now touched the leper and put the oil (on top of the blood) on the right ear, the thumb of the right hand and the great toe of the right foot. This was consecration indeed. He was sharing the blessing of the priesthood.

And yet there is more! The remainder of the oil in the vessel was now poured over the head of the man. But this was a ceremony carried out only for *the high priest* – not even for the priests, the sons of Aaron – and for prophets and for kings!

Forgiveness, healing and blessing are given in abundance by our God.

"Thou anointest my head with oil; my cup runneth over. Surely goodness and mercy shall follow me all the days of my life: and I will dwell in the house of the LORD for ever." (Psalm 23:5,6)

May we this day, the healed, cleansed and anointed lepers, as we meet in the presence of our high priest and before the tokens of his love, truly remember and praise our God and our Saviour and take this consecration into our homes and our lives with thankfulness and praise.

9

"GOD, BE MERCIFUL TO ME ..."
16th March

Leviticus 24   Psalms 131-134   **Luke 7**

OF the many occasions on which Jesus met and talked with sinners, one of the most moving is that recorded in Luke 7. It is not difficult to picture Jesus reclining at a meal in the Pharisee's house, and becoming the subject of an anointing performed with a depth of love and submission that overflowed with tears. The Pharisee was embarrassed, and said within himself: "This man, if he were a prophet, would have known who and what manner of woman this is that toucheth him: for she is a sinner" (verse 39). What a delightful situation! The enchantment of the scene lies in the fact that Jesus was fully aware of the woman's sins, and was respondent to the yearnings of her heart. "Her sins, which are many, are forgiven; for she loved much ..."

The sinner, whose loathsomeness was known of men, and abhorred of God, was transformed by the washing of repentance: and, while she washed and anointed the feet of her Saviour, he made her wholly clean by a love which exceeded even her own. The Pharisee was shortsighted. He saw only a 'leprous' woman before him, whose past life was calling "Unclean! Unclean!" In his ignorance he failed to see the significance of the testimony that the whole world lieth in wickedness and there is none clean, no, not one.

Jesus made it perfectly clear in his preaching that his sole desire was to save sinners: "I came not to call the righteous, but sinners to repentance." This was a mystery to the self-righteous. Only those, like the woman who was a sinner, who seeing the glory of God in the face of Jesus Christ, had fallen before him in confession of their sins, could be healed by the great physician. "They that are whole need not a physician; but they that are sick" (Luke 5:31,32). The Pharisee knew not that in the eyes of God his

47

self-righteousness was but the empty boast of health by a man who was a leper. God, through Jesus, was seeking for those who were willing to confess their need of healing – and not one would be turned away. Jesus was seeking these words from the hearts of his hearers: "If thou wilt, thou canst make me clean". And, immediately, there would come the glorious, regenerating finger of God: "I will: be thou clean".

Wherever we turn among the righteous men and women of scripture, we find that this consciousness of sin and the need for mercy is the secret of their humility and service. This is the common bond between all brethren and sisters the world over and through all ages, and it was shared by Jesus to the extent that he was made in the likeness of sinful flesh, against which the Spirit of his Father made continual warfare.

Examples of Confession

Three simple examples of confession will drive home the lesson and call us to the ranks of those whom God can heal. Listen to Isaiah, as he cries, "I am undone", as recorded in his sixth chapter:

"I am undone; because I am a man of unclean lips, and I dwell in the midst of a people of unclean lips ..."

(verse 5)

Peter, lovable and forthright, makes his admission of guilt in the presence of the righteous Son of God:

"He fell down at Jesus' knees, saying, Depart from me; for I am a sinful man, O Lord." (Luke 5:8)

Finally, Paul, ever conscious of his merciless persecution of the church of God, cries out to Timothy:

"This is a faithful saying, and worthy of all acceptation, that Christ Jesus came into the world to save sinners; of whom I am chief." (1 Timothy 1:15)

These are the words of God's beloved ones, and because of their self-effacement, great things were done by Him through them. For – and let there be no mistake about this – God did not desire and did not receive a mere abject grovelling heap of misery at His feet when each of these saints made confession to Him. There was a reason for the confession, and in that lay the true nobility of character of

48

His servants. It was the desire for righteousness which brought them to confession. If we examine carefully the words of the sinner in Christ's parable, the object of confession will be at once apparent: "God be merciful to me, a sinner." It is the cry for mercy, for healing, for salvation which brings the love of God into the heart of the individual. When Jesus used the word "merciful" in the parable he used the word which is essentially connected with propitiation and reconciliation. The sinner desired to be in harmony with God. He yearned for the righteous garments of God that he might appear in God's family. Jesus gives the assurance: "I tell you, this man went down to his house justified rather than the other" (Luke 18:13,14).

Accounted righteous

The Saviour's choice of the word "justified", is especially apt. It means 'accounted righteous'. The sinner, upon confession of his utter reliance upon God, went home clothed in righteousness. That is our position in Christ Jesus, and it is to remember the greatness of the work of Jesus to this end that we assemble to break bread and drink wine. However lonely our life in the Truth, let us never forget that God has given to us His own clothing – Jesus the righteousness of God. Were there ever garments like these? Let us come before Him and bow the knee.

"Not unto us, who are but dust,
But unto Thee is glory due."   (Hymn 56, verse 1)

Yes, that is the spirit. If we can hold that, we have the secret of true confession and its true motive power.

The Psalmist with delightful simplicity of language writes: "There is forgiveness with thee, that thou mayest be feared" (Psalm 130:4). Forgiveness is not an end in itself, it is the means to an end – the fear of Him who has redeemed us by the precious blood of His only-begotten Son. Anyone living in that attitude of mind is never self-reliant but always leaning upon Him. You will remember the figure in the Song of Solomon where we read:

"Who is this that cometh up from the wilderness,
leaning upon her beloved?"   (8:5)

49

Desire forgiveness

Let us, then, be unrestrained in our confession to Him. Open the floodgates and seek relief. How foolish we are – it surely applies to every one of us at times – in containing our sins within us and refusing to seek relief in Him. Why is it? Do we think that our sins are so utterly vile that there cannot possibly be forgiveness in our case? The writer to the Hebrews is confident that Christ is able to save to the uttermost (7:25) – and that means us. David once tried to live without confession, and later he wrote:

"When I kept silence, my bones waxed old through my roaring all the day long. For day and night thy hand was heavy upon me: my moisture is turned into the drought of summer." (Psalm 32:3,4)

If that is our condition at this moment let us forsake our foolishness and come unto Him. It cannot be that He will turn us away. If we seek unto Him we shall find that He is already halfway down the road to meet us – as the father was for the prodigal son. The everlasting springs of God's mercy are able to satisfy our thirst, but we must come to the waters to drink. We cannot gaze upon them from afar and hope that our parched throats will feel cool and refreshed. The call is to taste and see that the Lord is good. Come, then, and let us go to the waters of forgiveness; kneel down beside them, bow the head and drink. "As cold waters to a thirsty soul, so is good news from a far country." God has given to us the good news and brought us to Him from afar. Let us then acknowledge Him in all our ways, and He will direct our steps. Our Father desires to separate us from our sins and, like so many paradoxes in God's ways, the confession of our weakness is the opportunity for strength.

"Behold, the eye of the LORD is upon them that fear him, upon them that hope in his mercy." (Psalm 33:18)

As strong as is our desire for forgiveness, just so great is the forgiveness; as much as we hope for mercy, so much do we receive it.

Confidence and warning

There is one final aspect of this matter which gives us confidence and warning. Let us first consider the warning, and take heed. Putting the matter in its bluntest terms – the terms which the scripture uses – if we fail to confess our sins we make a liar of God. You will remember the words in 1 John 1: "If we say that we have not sinned, we make him a liar, and his word is not in us". No brother or sister would be heard saying, "I am sinless" – the idea is too ridiculous. But, says John, if you are one of those people who refrain from good and honest confession, then you are saying to God: "I have no sin". And that is mocking Him and making Him a liar, for He has recorded that if we say that we have no sin, we deceive ourselves, and the truth is not in us. So much for the warning – let us never imagine for one moment that we can treat lightly the extended hand of God.

Now let us look at the confidence which John is assured of and confirms in his first epistle:

"My little children, these things write I unto you, that ye sin not. And if any man sin, we have an advocate with the Father, Jesus Christ the righteous." (2:1)

Perhaps of all the works of Christ this is the most neglected. Yet apart from the glorious work of this heavenly high priest there is no hope for the saints. What does John mean when he says that we have an advocate with the Father? What is an advocate, and how is the term applicable to Jesus? A little careful examination with the aid of a concordance reveals hidden beauties – like shy violets in the hedgerow whose beauty is revealed only to the observant and the seeking. The word "advocate" is exactly the same word which is translated "comforter" in the Gospel of John. "We have a comforter with the Father", is the meaning of the phrase. And the comfort which the compassionate, understanding and all-powerful Son of God can render is absolutely beyond comparison.

The faltering confession of the poor saint is taken by the able-to-save-to-the-uttermost Comforter, who pours sweet consolation into the heart of the confessor, and presents his petition to the Father with groanings which cannot be uttered. Was there ever a privilege like this? That a poor mortal, who is but dust and ashes, should have ever at his side the resplendent and sympathetic Son of God. How is it then that we so often fail to see him? Why do we persist in carrying our burden of woe?

Let us be ever confident of this one thing – he understands us completely and his one great desire is to help us. We frustrate that loving compassion only in so far as we fail to ask for it. If he had asked some great thing from us, would we not have done it? Let us then humble ourselves under the mighty hand of God, and seek for His mercy in prayer. There can be no doubt about the fact that the fervent prayer of a righteous man evokes a response from heaven. As the angels rejoice over one sinner that repenteth, and as our angels always behold the face of our Father in heaven, so surely does the Father Himself respond to our cry.

In isolation

No brother or sister is in isolation. It is impossible to be isolated from God. The softest breath of prayer is heard by the ever-present Jesus, and the angels are his constant messengers attending to the ministry of the saints.

When our loneliness seems too much for us to bear, and our strength is weaker than that of a newborn babe, let us remember that just at that moment Christ can help us most. His strength is made perfect in weakness. Bend the reluctant knee and yield to him in prayer. The answer will astound us. He can give above all that we can ask or think, and not one saint is outside his power. As you take the bread between your fingers, and as the wine passes between your lips, consider and know that the Father and Son are as near as the emblems; yea, they have promised that they will come and make their abode with us:

"I said, I will confess my transgressions unto the LORD; and thou forgavest the iniquity of my sin. For this shall every one that is godly pray unto thee in a time when thou mayest be found." (Psalm 32:5,6)

10

"HE IS RISEN"

1st April

Numbers 15   Proverbs 11   **Luke 24**

D URING the three days of waiting, different persons and different groups of people were doing widely different things. The disciples were afraid for their lives. Peter was in the darkest despair and desolation of spirit. The women were anxious to do the right things about the body of Jesus, and purchased the appropriate ointment and spices to do their work of love; having forgotten that the work of love had already been done when Mary anointed him six days before the Passover (John 12:1-7).

The Father was silent. The angels were waiting. The Lord rested on the sabbath day. The Pharisees had set their guard and made the tomb as secure as they could.

For Pilate it was the end of a routine job but not the last he would hear of this Jesus of Nazareth.

The key scriptures were about to speak, for had not Christ died according to the scriptures and would he not rise again according to the scriptures? These scriptures were quoted and alluded to by Jesus himself and the apostles. On the day of Pentecost, Peter cited the Psalms of David as evidence for the resurrection:

"Thou wilt not leave my soul in hell, neither wilt thou suffer thine Holy One to see corruption."

(Acts 2:27, quoting Psalm 16:10)

Jesus referred to the experience of Jonah and used it as a parable:

"For as Jonas was three days and three nights in the whale's belly; so shall the Son of man be three days and three nights in the heart of the earth." (Matthew 12:40)

So Jesus foretold that which would shortly come upon him; how that he would be three days and three nights in the heart of the earth and would rise again – to proclaim (through his witnesses) the gospel to the Gentiles.

Paul, in speaking of "the firstfruits of them that slept" (1 Corinthians 15:20), was bringing to mind the wave sheaf of the firstfruits that was offered on the morning after the sabbath (Leviticus 23:11). Again Paul says that Jesus "rose again the third day according to the scriptures" (verse 4). The passage in question is surely that found in Hosea:

"After two days will he revive us: in the third day he will raise us up, and we shall live in his sight."

(Hosea 6:2)

Surprised by Joy

In secret, the Lord had risen and the angel had descended; there had been an earthquake and the stone was rolled away, and the angel sat upon it. The guards were stricken and afraid. They trembled greatly and fell as though they were dead. The worthless seal of the authorities was broken that the word of God might be kept.

It was all reminiscent of another tomb – a lion's den which was covered at its mouth by a stone and sealed with the king's own signet. Darius in his anxiety had come on the morning after to say:

"O Daniel, servant of the living God, is thy God, whom thou servest continually, able to deliver thee from the lions?" (Daniel 6:20)

Now the greater than Daniel ('God is Judge') was delivered from the mouth of the lion. Him had God the Father sealed and the word had been spoken:

"Mercy and truth are met together;
Righteousness and peace have kissed each other.
Truth shall spring out of the earth;
And righteousness shall look down from heaven."

(Psalm 85:10,11)

"(He) who was delivered for our offences, and was raised again for our justification." (Romans 4:25)

Sinful Adam's journey to death and the grave was retraced by sinlessness and faith:

"O death, where is thy sting? O grave, where is thy victory?" (1 Corinthians 15:55)

This is our comfort at every brother or sister's grave side; it is the assurance above all human conjectures and speculations. It is the truth.

"Therefore, my beloved brethren, be ye stedfast, unmoveable, always abounding in the work of the Lord, forasmuch as ye know that your labour is not in vain in the Lord." (verse 58)

But all of this was hidden from the women's view as they journeyed to the tomb, walking in literal darkness, wondering how the stone could be removed to let them in to perform their works of tender love amidst their bitter tears. The sun rose as they neared the place, bearing their now needless burdens of spices and ointments. Instead of a stone there was a doorway. Like so many instances in our pilgrim lives, the seeming roadblocks to our journey become the open portals of access to greater joy and service.

He is Risen!

But the open door had not removed their fears. Who possibly could have entered the tomb before them? What wicked work had been done to their helpless Lord? Their problem had been to get into the tomb; the great problem for mankind was how to come out. The open tomb was the sign that *someone* had come forth. "Thoroughly nonplussed" (much perplexed) they entered and saw the greatest vacant space there has ever yet been on earth. Never had anyone seen *nothing* with so much import!

Two dazzling angels then revealed themselves, terrifying the women and then asking the most wonderful of all questions:

"Why seek ye the living among the dead? He is not here, but is risen: remember how he spake unto you when he was yet in Galilee, saying, The Son of man must be delivered into the hands of sinful men, and be crucified, and the third day rise again." (Luke 24:5-7)

What a morning. Where did they leave the spices? The party of women numbering at least five hurried to the company of believers – "the eleven, and to all the rest" – to tell them the good news. No one believed them. We can imagine the scene: a party of greatly excited, amazed, breathless women with a story that probably seemed to be incoherent, and was certainly beyond the listeners' belief. Their talk seemed as "twaddle" (Strong's).

Nevertheless, Peter ran to find out: the tomb was open and empty, and, moreover, the linen clothes had been left behind! He returned marvelling at what he had seen.

Wondering still

Other things, not recorded by Luke, happened during the day; but he alone relates the account of two disciples journeying homeward, having heard the story of the women and of those (therefore, more than just Peter) who ran to the tomb, but were still sad and disbelieving. The record tells us that the two disciples were "communicating" one with another. The word means to 'knock to and fro'; 'to bandy'.

Jesus comes upon them and asks why they are so sad and troubled. "They stood still" (RV); they couldn't believe that anyone who had been in Jerusalem, unless he be a stranger living alone, could possibly not know "what things" they were talking about.

Succinctly, they say precisely what had happened to Jesus. They lay the blame entirely on "the chief priests and our rulers", and give never a mention to the part played by Rome. In deep desolation they say, "But we trusted that it had been he which should have redeemed Israel". They believed the promises and that Jesus had been their hoped-for Messiah.

These things should warn us in our own day. They had heads full of scriptures and hearts full of love for Christ, but they could not see what the implications of these things were from the events of the day. How could they be so blind? Take care; it was the Pharisees who, in another connection, said:

"If we had been in the days of our fathers, we would not have been partakers with them in the blood of the prophets."   (Matthew 23:30)

Sometimes events are too big for our little minds to grasp, too wonderful for us to sort them out for what they are. God leads us by the hand and will not let us go, even though we are slow of heart to believe. Things are going to happen in our day, things that are clear precursors of the Lord's coming, and we shall be inclined to miss them or to misinterpret them. With hindsight we shall see that they were shouting their message from the house tops, but had been heard but dimly.

"Beside all this, today is the third day since these things were done". Not even that word and the women's message and the empty tomb and the grave clothes could take the veil from their eyes. It required the patient exposition of scripture: not a vision, not "It is I", but the Master's "expounding" (explaining thoroughly) of the word of God.

Oh, to have been there as the Christ became plain in living, dying and rising again from the master touch of the word of God. The furlongs had slipped away as they resumed their walk and evening was drawing on. He would have pressed on but they urged him to abide with them. ("Be not forgetful to entertain strangers: for thereby some have entertained angels unawares.") He was persuaded and they reclined for their evening meal.

Their guest was quietly transformed into the host. He reached forward and took the loaf in his hands, and offered a prayer in blessing. As he passed the loaf – either in seeing his hands or in sudden recollection of times past – they knew him. Before they could speak or worship or cry for joy or be afraid or ashamed, he was gone. The bread was still there, but things were different. Their hearts had burned within them; a fire had been kindled that was unquenchable.

Every breaking of bread has its recollection of that time. We too meet and beseech him to abide with us. "Where two or three are gathered together in my name, there am I in the midst of them." Though we see him not, and are awaiting his return, yet our hearts burn within us. We too are amongst the believing and remembering throng that this day calls to mind and to which it looks forward.

Quickly, that very hour, they set forth on the return journey to Jerusalem. Once more the eleven and the others are there and, before they can commence their own wonderful tale, they are told that they also know that the Lord is risen indeed and that he had appeared to Simon.

And then, right in the middle of their conversation and in their very midst, stood the Lord himself. "Peace be unto you" fell on frightened ears. This was a spirit – how could it be the Christ?

There is something delightful in their lack of presumption. Who were they that the Lord should visit them? So awesome a thought did not occur to them. But their cup was to be filled to overflowing. They were invited to touch him. Who amongst us would have dared? Shyly, fearfully, wonderfully, they touched him – perhaps with eyes that never raised themselves to see his face. Unworthy creatures, men who had forsaken him and fled, one who had denied him, all who had never loved enough stood around in deep wondering. What was there to say or to do? No one since creation had ever been in such a situation.

The Lord knew and brought them to a gentle realisation as he ate fish and honey. He ate for them – he who now needed nothing. The fish were for the fishermen and for fishers of men.

Once more he expounded and opened the scriptures. Food for fishermen, honey to their taste! "Thus it is written" was the basis of their conviction. Now they knew that the sufferings were the forerunners of the glory. Moreover he was now indubitably their saviour from sin and death, and they were to take the good news to the nations.

Here then, is the conviction in our gathering together. The living word flowed out of Zion and brought fire to our hearts. We know how he expounded the word because the apostles have passed it on to us in all they said and wrote.

As they worshipped and returned with joy, so we assemble and pour out our hearts before the Father and His beloved Son. The Lord is risen indeed.

11

THE LORD OF LIFE
18th April

Deuteronomy 1   Proverbs 28   **John 11**

JESUS is on the far side of Jordan where John first baptized in Bethabara (John 10:40; 1:28). This is the land "beyond Jordan", identified by Josephus as Perea, where Jesus went following his discourse on the Good Shepherd and his witness that he was the Son of God.

In the village of Bethany, two miles or so from Jerusalem, disaster has struck the family of Martha, Mary and Lazarus. Fatal illness had beset Lazarus. The faithful three had but one recourse – the Master.

Would that we found ourselves so promptly conscious of our Lord at all times. They seem to have known where Christ was and sent a messenger to him: "He whom thou lovest is sick" ("lovest" is the word of intimacy, *phileo*). There was no request for the Lord to come – at least not directly.

The Lord's Response

The message is known to the disciples and Jesus tells them that the sickness is not unto death, but for the glory of God that the Son of God might be glorified thereby. Here was encapsulated in the death of Lazarus and his being raised from the dead, the battle of Christ against sin and death, and his glorious rising again.

The Final Victory

Lazarus' name means 'God is my Helper', from the Greek equivalent for Eleazar, the name of the High Priest. The love of Jesus (verse 5) for the family was expressed by the Greek *agape*. It went beyond the intimate human love to the quality of God's own love for us.

We know from verse 17 that in all probability Lazarus was already dead by the time the messenger found Jesus. Jesus knew too. He remained for two more days and then journeyed to Bethany. The disciples were fearful for his safety after the threat of stoning by the Jews (10:31), but needed to learn that the day's work had to be done during the day. News ran ahead of Jesus.

We too must learn that, as children of light, as children of the day, we must do the work of the day. Night is coming – our own night of death, and the night when the work will cease when the Lord comes as a thief in the night.

"Our Friend Lazarus"

Even when dead, Lazarus is spoken of by Jesus as his friend. Herein is hope and comfort. Naboth's vineyard was still called the vineyard of Naboth by God even when Naboth had been stoned. Friends of God are His eternal friends. "There is a friend that sticketh closer than a brother".

"Our friend Lazarus sleepeth" – he has fallen asleep. The same expression is found in Paul's letters:

"And if Christ be not raised, your faith is vain; ye are yet in your sins. Then they also which are fallen *asleep in Christ* are perished ... But now is Christ risen from the dead, and become the firstfruits of them that slept."
(1 Corinthians 15:17,18,20)

"For if we believe that Jesus died and rose again, even so them also which *sleep in Jesus* will God bring with him." (1 Thessalonians 4:14)

On this eventful journey Jesus "himself knew what he would do" (see John 6:6). Christ had agonized in prayer and was prepared for everything, though some of it would cost him dearly.

Near to Bethany

As he nears Bethany, Martha gets to know and immediately leaves everything to go to Jesus. In Luke 10 she had been cumbered (distracted) with much serving, but now she is free from everything but her faith in Christ.

If only the Lord had been there, her brother would not have died. His healing hand would surely have touched him, and even now, what the Lord might ask of his Father would be granted. Just what she had in mind is difficult to say in view of her reluctance later on to have the grave opened, but she had faith in Christ and knew that his power came from God.

The Lord's answer contained all – so we now know by hindsight – but he could have been talking about the ultimate resurrection so far as Martha was concerned. It is surprising how all of us fail to see the Lord near at hand even though we are certain of his coming again. We defer some of our happiness unnecessarily. He never leaves us or forsakes us, for we are his friends if we seek to do whatsoever he has commanded us.

"Thy brother shall rise again"

The expression "rise again" (John 11:23) is the same as that found in John 6:39,40,44,54; 11:24,31; 20:9. And, like our word 'rise' it has more than one meaning, including in the right context, rising from the dead. Martha had heard the words of Jesus on this very subject and she knew – she perceived fully – that Christ would raise the dead at the last day. The message of John 6:39 etc. had been preached to her and she was confident in it, and said so.

Jesus proceeded to educate her further even in this time of distress. He himself, mortal as he was and not yet perfected, embodied the total hope: he was the resurrection and the life. This subject had been opened up in John 5. We live in Christ and we die in him. The fulness of those words does not always register with us. As we saw in 1 Thessalonians 4, even those that sleep in Jesus will God bring with him.

God had given Christ the Spirit without measure; it made it possible for him to raise the dead. He had within him the power to give life and soon would have the power to give it eternally. Meanwhile for all who are dead in trespasses and sins he has the power to quicken them to a new life. Moreover, he can bring the dead to life and preserve the faithful living to eternity. No one who believes in him will "die unto the age", or, as some versions have it, "die for ever".

Unknown to Martha, though she must have been aware that something was to happen, the Lord was both educating her and preparing her for the forthcoming wonder. As with the woman at the well and the blind man in Jerusalem, the Lord evoked a confession from Martha – the very essence of true faith:

> "Yea, Lord: I believe [have believed] that thou art the Christ, the Son of God, which should come into the world." (John 11:27)

This is a confession of the truth of the Old Testament, of the Messiahship of the Lord Jesus, and therefore that he was Son of God.

Now it was Mary's turn. Secretly Martha tells her of the Lord's approach and she hastens to him, and falls down at his feet – the position she had adopted when she had sat listening to him while Martha laboured (Luke 10:39). The mourners had trailed her and saw it all.

She repeats the words which she and her sister must have said time and again:

> "Lord, if thou hadst been here, my brother had not died." (John 11:32)

The word for "weeping" here (verse 33) is 'wailing' in which both Martha and the mourners engaged. Jesus "groaned". It is a word which elsewhere is used when the Lord was angry. Literally, it means to snort, when applied to horses, and to be deeply moved when applied to men. His spirit was troubled within.

Many ideas have been suggested as explanation of what the Lord did. Perhaps he resented the hypocrisy of the paid mourners, or the unbelief of so many people, or the evil of death. None of them seems to ring one hundred per cent true, which may be because it is beyond our understanding. Maybe the Lord felt strongly about sin by which death had come into the world and was bracing himself for the time when he must bind Satan in his own house.

At the tomb he wept, not wailed – wept in common sorrow at the necessary distress of the family, even though he was shortly to transform the scene into one of joy. This strange mixture of being of us and yet of the Father is more than we are able to understand.

The people around reflected on his past miracles and they too wondered why he had not intervened in the sickness of Lazarus. No one perceived the wonder of what was about to happen, a miracle at the very heart of the ultimate power of Christ.

He commanded the stone to be moved away. Martha, ever practical, warned against the corruption that must already have set in. He reminds her, seemingly of verse 4 which must have been conveyed as part of the reply to their telegraphic message:

"Said I not unto thee, that, if thou wouldest believe, thou shouldest see the glory of God?" (verse 40)

No human hands would remove the stone of his tomb and no stone would prevent his coming forth.

At the door of the sepulchre the Lord prayed a prayer of thankfulness and praise in total confidence, that what he was about to do had already been granted by his Father. Maybe we have assumed that his miracles were always wrought as spontaneous acts, as though drawing on a reservoir of internal power. But he has told us that some miracles required prayer and fasting. He must have been ever thankful, ever beseeching and ever believing as he did his mighty works.

He prayed aloud, not for show, but to tell the people beforehand that his work was the work of God. The great cry to Lazarus echoed around. Earlier Martha had said to Mary, "The Master (Teacher) is come and calleth for thee". And, now it was being said again in effect to the apparently deaf ears of Lazarus.

There was no sudden striding forth from the tomb. Maybe it was a shuffle towards the light as a man bound hand and foot in grave clothes, with a napkin (sweatcloth) about his head, slowly made his way out. "Loose him, and let him go", was willingly obeyed. 'God is my helper' stood amongst them alive.

It was, of course, a mixed blessing. Lazarus had died in faith and under normal conditions his next conscious moment would have been the resurrection at the last day. Now he came forth to the joy of his family and to the hatred of the Lord's enemies who would seek to reverse the miracle by putting Lazarus to death.

In our prayers we look for blessings of certain kinds without sometimes weighing up the full consequences of what we are asking. Life is not everything. It must end in any case. Death in Christ is better than life without him. But God had a purpose for the risen Lazarus to fulfil and we shall have to wait until the kingdom to find out what it was.

The Division

The true reading of verse 45 conveys the idea that all of those Jews who came to Mary to comfort her believed in the miracle of Christ. Other Jews quenched their possibility of faith in him by reporting the occurrence to the Pharisees. Even these people could not deny the wonderful event, but they denied the Lord himself. He had warned in the parable of the Rich Man and Lazarus that they would not believe though one rose from the dead. We sometimes think that miracles would convince even the stony-hearted, but it is not so. Faith has to grow from a good and honest heart.

The Pharisees told the Sadducees who immediately convened the Sanhedrin to discuss what had to be done. Their status, wealth and position in the nation meant more to them than the Christ. These choices occur every day. For Judas it was thirty pieces of silver, for Ananias and Sapphira it was sham faith; for others it is their job, their money, wrong companions, negligence, love of pleasure. Beware!

Caiaphas, now the infamous (a name like Pilate's, remembered only because of the wicked part played in the death of Christ), was astute and ruthless. The man who raised the dead, healed the leper, fed the poor, was a cheap price to pay to Rome. A few well-placed words would deprive the cowardly Pilate of his conscience. A rent-a-mob cry would ensure the choice of Barabbas, and it would all be over – but Caiaphas did not know that meant the end of Judah's commonwealth and not of Christ.

Caiaphas became a prophet to speak words he thought he understood, but like those given to Balaam, were fitted with eternal wings:

"The Lord GOD which gathereth the outcasts of Israel saith, Yet will I gather others to him, beside those that are gathered unto him." (Isaiah 56:8, cp. John 11:52)

The Good Shepherd of John 10 had other sheep, a Gentile flock, to bring unto himself. Caiaphas unwittingly spoke of them and of the One Redeemer for the chosen race of God. The One Death would secure their place and nation, a place and a name better than that of sons, and a nation of king-priests in which Caiaphas and his ilk would have no part.

Cana of Galilee had begun to show forth the glory of Christ and of his Father; the day of Lazarus was harbinger of the final glory when the Father would be glorified in the Son and the Son would be glorified by the Father.

As yet another occasion presents itself for us to remember what has been achieved on our behalf, it cannot be long now before the Lord comes again to the house of those who mourn to comfort them. We too will hear the words, "The Master is come, and calleth for thee". May we find him to be for us the Resurrection and the Life.

COMFORT OF THE SCRIPTURES

12

THOUGHTS ON THE BRIDE
9th May
Deuteronomy 26   **Song of Solomon 6**   Acts 21,22

WE sometimes get lost in the imagery of the Song of Solomon and fail to take to heart some of the basically simple and saving lessons that are to be found there. Today we shall look at some of the things concerning the Bride, arising in the first place from the reading for today.

Here is the description of the Bride:

"Who is she that looketh forth as the morning, fair as the moon, clear as the sun, and terrible as an army with banners?"   (Song of Solomon 6:10)

This is the collective bride as the conclusion of the verse would indicate. But look at some of the qualities she possesses.

Looketh forth

It is as though she looks down from her window at the breaking of the day. She is a bride of the morning: early morning, the dawn. She is waiting for Zion's glad morning when she will meet her beloved. We are people of the day, people of the light, those of whom it is said:

"The path of the just is as the shining light, that shineth more and more unto the perfect day."
(Proverbs 4:18)

The perfect day is the dawn. Our deeds are to be deeds of light and not works of darkness. We must be lookout people, watching:

"My soul waiteth for the Lord more than they that watch for the morning: I say, more than they that watch for the morning."   (Psalm 130:6)

The Bride was looking out for the coming of her Lord. So are we.

Fair as the Moon

The symbolism of scripture often makes Christ the Sun (of righteousness, for example) and the orb of reflected light, the Moon, is the Bride. She is white, like the snow of Lebanon (for such is the word used for the moon in Song of Solomon 6:10). We must seek to be snow white and beyond reproach in this world of debased morals. Amongst ourselves too we must behave in that way.

You will recall that scripture says of the Bride that her clothing is both "white" and "clean":

"Let us be glad and rejoice, and give honour to him: for the marriage of the Lamb is come, and his wife hath made herself ready. And to her was granted that she should be arrayed in fine linen, clean and white: for the fine linen is the righteousness of saints."

(Revelation 19:7,8)

The Bride makes herself ready; that is the part of every bride. In response to her preparation God's gift to her is that she will be clothed in fine linen, clean and pure. She will be clothed with righteousness because she has kept her trust with the Bridegroom. The Psalmist gives the same message:

"Who shall ascend into the hill of the LORD? or who shall stand in his holy place? He that hath clean hands, and a pure heart; who hath not lifted up his soul unto vanity, nor sworn deceitfully. He shall receive the blessing from the LORD, and righteousness from the God of his salvation." (Psalm 24:3-5)

Clear as the Sun

"Clear" means 'clean, pure'. It occurs in the expression, "He that hath clean hands, and a pure heart". The Bride is chaste for her husband. This means that she has not dallied with other attractions, not sullied her mind, not betrayed her trust. As he is pure, so she seeks to be pure:

"For I am jealous over you with godly jealousy: for I have espoused you to one husband, that I may present you as a chaste (pure) virgin to Christ."

(2 Corinthians 11:2)

"These are they which were not defiled with women; for they are virgins. These are they which follow the

Lamb whithersoever he goeth ... And in their mouth was found no guile: for they are without fault before the throne of God." (Revelation 14:4,5)

Terrible as an Army with Banners

The Song pictures the collective bride as though she were a bannered host in powerful display. It is an image used elsewhere in the scriptures:

"We will rejoice in thy salvation, and in the name of our God we will set up our banners: the LORD fulfil all thy petitions." (Psalm 20:5)

"Thou hast given a banner to them that fear thee, that it may be displayed because of the truth." (Psalm 60:4)

"And Moses built an altar, and called the name of it Jehovah-nissi [The LORD my banner]." (Exodus 17:15)

This altar was built after and in connection with the command of the Lord to Moses to "Write this for a memorial in a book" (verse 14).

Here as we meet at the Lord's table are our great memorials, the banner over us and the flag we fly:

"He brought me to the banqueting house, and his banner over me was love." (Song of Solomon 2:4)

Others look for battle honours, the fading flag in some cathedral; but the saints are the host of peace, whose ensign is love.

The Chariots

"Or ever I was aware, my soul made me like the chariots of Amminadib." (Song of Solomon 6:12)

It is not wholly clear whether this verse is spoken by the Bride or the Groom. Different versions choose different solutions. Let us take it for our purposes that the reference is to the Bride. It is the last part of the verse which is intriguing – "chariots of Amminadib". Amminadib means 'my princely or my willing people'. The redeemed are called "princes" in Isaiah 32:1 and in Psalm 45:16, and they are called "willing" in Psalm 110:

"Thy people shall be willing in the day of thy power, in the beauties of holiness from the womb of the

69

morning: thou hast the dew of thy youth."

(Psalm 110:3)

And willingness is spoken of as that which marks out the true servants in other passages:

"Speak unto the children of Israel, that they bring me an offering: of every man that giveth it willingly with his heart ye shall take my offering." (Exodus 25:2)

"And they came, everyone whose heart stirred him up, and everyone whom his spirit made willing, and they brought the LORD's offering to the work of the tabernacle of the congregation, and for all his service, and for the holy garments." (Exodus 35:21)

"Praise ye the LORD for the avenging of Israel, when the people willingly offered themselves." (Judges 5:2)

"Then the people rejoiced, for that they offered willingly, because with perfect heart they offered willingly to the LORD: and David the king also rejoiced with great joy." (1 Chronicles 29:9)

These "willing servants" are also a "princely people" (as the Revised Version translates Amminadib). Again the nation's history provides the context. When God brought His people out of Egypt to see if they had willing hearts for His service, He wanted them to be a "kingdom of priests, and an holy nation" (Exodus 19:6). Their future exaltation lay in the relationship to which God was calling them. And we are no different.

The Song of Solomon is a rich vein of spiritual treasure, to be mined by those who are God's peculiar people, "called out of darkness into his marvellous light" (1 Peter 2:9). Through the language of the song, we are brought to see more clearly both the Bride and the Bridegroom, and to appreciate the love bestowed upon us while we were yet sinners. The same is true of the emblems we share: the loaf describes both the single-minded devotion of the Saviour and the unity he desires among his disciples; the wine represents his shed blood and that which makes glad the heart of his followers.

"My beloved spake, and said unto me, Rise up, my love, my fair one, and come away. For, lo, the winter is past." (Song of Solomon 2:10,11)

13

THE THINGS OF REDEMPTION
21st May

Joshua 7   **Isaiah 11**   **2 Thessalonians 3**

IT was not long since the trumpet blasts had died away and the great shout had rent the air. Jericho had fallen, all except the piece of wall on which stood Rahab's house in which was salvation for her and her family. The scarlet, redeeming thread had been the token of her faith and the sign to Israel that the house and family were the Lord's.

Jericho had been prosperous and wicked. They trafficked widely and dealt in goods from afar. Tempting as the spoil would be, nothing was to be taken for personal use. The living were to be slain and the silver, gold and vessels of brass and iron, were to be consecrated to the Lord (Joshua 6:18,19).

Jericho was "accursed" for we read:

"And the city shall be accursed, even it, and all that are therein, to the LORD: only Rahab the harlot shall live, she and all that are with her in the house, because she hid the messengers that we sent." (verse 17)

The word translated "accursed" can also have the meaning of 'devoted'. It is used, for example, in connection with offerings that were promised to Aaron and his sons:

"This shall be thine of the most holy things, reserved from the fire: every oblation of theirs, every meat offering of theirs, and every sin offering of theirs, and every trespass offering of theirs, which they shall render unto me, shall be most holy for thee and for thy sons ... Every thing devoted in Israel shall be thine." (Numbers 18:9,14)

Literally the word means 'excluded or under a ban'. Strong's definition has:

71

"A doomed object; dedicated thing; things which should have been utterly destroyed; (appointed to) utter destruction; devoted (thing); net."

In this case, God was to be sanctified by the extermination of evil. It was the beginning of His judgement on the Land. Only the things which could pass through the fire were to be retained, and then only for the Lord's use because they were holy to Him. Israel were to turn their eyes to the Lord and give all to Him. The Land was to be holy and the people were to be part of that holiness. Moreover, Jericho was the firstfruits of Israel's conquests and was wholly the Lord's.

The Sin of Achan

The conquest of Jericho was accomplished by all of the people – the ecclesia of God as a whole was involved. It was one work, by the one people; it was one victory. Similarly, it was one responsibility: any failure was the failure of all.

Apparently without seeking the Lord in prayer, the spies were sent out and returned to say that taking Ai would be the simple task of two or three thousand men. But they failed and thirty-six died. Joshua was devastated. Had God forsaken them? What then of the fame of the Name of the Lord?

But the fault lay in Israel – they had forfeited God's blessing. The solemn assembly of the ritually cleansed or sanctified people was a fearful moment. The moment had come for the wrongdoer to be exposed.

Unerringly the Spirit, perhaps indicating by the Urim and Thummim, revealed the tribe, the family, the household and finally the man – the offshoot of Achan was isolated. His sin was confessed; the Lord had said that the sinner had wrought "folly" in Israel (Joshua 7:15), a word reserved for serious sin as, for example, with Dinah and Tamar. The guilty secret exposed, men were sent to retrieve the hidden booty and Achan and his family had nowhere to hide.

He had broken the covenant of the Lord by deliberately flouting a specific command, but he had also coveted and stolen the Lord's goods, thus breaking the eighth and the tenth commandments.

All for his life

By a strange coincidence the word used in 7:1 for Achan's sin – "took" – is the same in the Septuagint as is used for the deceit of Ananias and Sapphira – "kept back" – (Acts 5:2,3). The root Greek word in both instances is *nosphi*, meaning to sequestrate for oneself, to embezzle, to keep back, to purloin. Will a man rob God? Truly, because he has done it throughout all mortal time. Will a man rob God and keep the thing hidden from Him? Never!

What had he taken?

The spoils included a goodly Babylonish garment, two hundred shekels of silver and fifty shekels of gold in the form of a wedge (tongue). His heart had gone back to the very plain of Shinar, the place of Babel, of Nimrod and of Babylon. Destined to be destroyed by fire, this mantle had been removed in direct breach of the Lord's command. It was a mantle such as kings and prophets wore, a garment doubtless of some beauty and elegance. But it was Babylonish, and no doubt tainted with images from the land of idolatry.

Two hundred shekels of silver

Silver was used for the redemption money. Israel were a redeemed people and the tabernacle had its important parts resting in sockets of silver. But the blood of the redemption had been spurned and counted an unholy thing. To Achan it was but a light thing and he preferred the lust of his flesh and lust of his eyes.

A fifty-shekel piece of gold

This material, often used as a token of tried faith and immortality, would have fulfilled its role had it found its way into the service of the tabernacle as God intended. Instead, the greed for gold had corrupted a man's heart and thirty-six men had died.

And all of this was hidden in the earth. The sinner had hidden his Lord's money. "Out of thine own mouth will I judge thee". He stood condemned; his name was written in earth and not on earth.

Achan's wickedness incriminated his family who doubtless were aware of what he had done. Everything belonging to Achan was assembled – people, cattle and goods. All were destroyed as the scriptures witness:

"And Joshua, and all Israel with him, took Achan the son of Zerah, and the silver, and the garment, and the wedge of gold, and his sons, and his daughters, and his oxen, and his asses, and his sheep, and his tent, and all that he had: and they brought them unto the valley of Achor. And Joshua said, Why hast thou troubled us? the LORD shall trouble thee this day. And all Israel stoned him with stones, and burned them with fire, after they had stoned them with stones." (7:24,25)

"Did not Achan the son of Zerah commit a trespass in the accursed thing, and wrath fell on all the congregation of Israel? and that man perished not alone in his iniquity." (22:20)

"And the sons of Carmi; Achar, the troubler of Israel, who transgressed in the thing accursed."
(1 Chronicles 2:7)

The Principles

The principles carry through to New Testament times and beyond. "The Man of Sin" will be judged severely when the time is ripe. Our ecclesias must observe the lessons and not knowingly harbour that which is evil. Those who violate traditions (the things handed to us from the apostles) and those who are disorderly must be expelled. Otherwise our sins will spread like a canker and others will become involved. So we are commanded in our third reading in 2 Thessalonians 3:

"Now we command you, brethren, in the name of our Lord Jesus Christ, that ye withdraw yourselves from every brother that walketh disorderly, and not after the tradition which he received of us ... And if any man obey not our word by this epistle, note that man, and have no company with him, that he may be ashamed."
(verses 6,14)

We too will have to stand in the Judgement, that great day of sifting, when the Lord Jesus Christ will judge with righteousness; he will not judge after the sight of his eyes or reprove after the hearing of his ears.

When all that happens we shall, like Achan, be on the threshold of the kingdom. Christ will be here. He who was the ensign of the people at Calvary, when he was high and lifted up, will then be an ensign for the nations. He will recover the outcasts of Israel and establish the highway from Egypt to Assyria.

Then shall the saints cry out joyfully when all of their hopes are fulfilled and Zion's controversies are settled once and for all:

"Cry out and shout, thou inhabitant (inhabitress) of Zion: for great is the Holy One of Israel in the midst of thee."   (Isaiah 12:6)

COMFORT OF THE SCRIPTURES

14

"LET US RUN ..."

5th June

Joshua 23,24   Isaiah 29   **Hebrews 12**

EBREWS chapter 12 is contingent upon the previous chapter. The opening word of chapter 12 makes the link with what has gone before. "Wherefore" means "consequently" or "therefore". Because of what we have read in Hebrews 11, *therefore*, we are to "run with patience the race that is set before us" (12:1).

The Cloud of Witnesses

Some of the words and phrases in these early verses need explanation. "Compassed about" means 'they are about us' (there is another word for "totally surrounded"). The word can have two meanings: 'lie around' and 'hamper'. The latter is illustrated in the same letter:

"He himself also is compassed with infirmity."   (5:2)

We have no doubt about the witnesses. Knowledge of them for the believer is inescapable. Paul calls them forth as witnesses, a cloud of them.

The word "cloud" implies 'a dense throng of people'; in other words there is a great crowd of them. Whether it is to be taken in the special senses attached to 1 Thessalonians 4:17 and Revelation 1:7 (in these and similar verses a different word with the same meaning is used: Liddell and Scott make the words virtually interchangeable), is a point for discussion.

The word "Witnesses" has been the subject of much discussion as to whether it means 'spectators' as in the arena for the games, or in the more familiar Biblical sense of having been a witness for God. Much as the spectator interpretation is encouraging, it is not true in fact. The witnesses are not alive and watching, nor can we receive any encouragements directly from them, except in the example and victory which we find in them, and that derives from the Biblical meaning of witness.

77

Are the Witnesses Discouraging?

Sometimes we find ourselves discouraged by the mighty witnesses, and feel that they are above our grasp, beyond our being able to imitate them. Could we all be Abrahams and Daniels?

However, a reflective look at the witnesses in Hebrews 11 tells us more than the mighty feats of individuals; it picks out instead the seemingly ordinary things which they did as acts of faith.

Abel did what he had been told, doubtless by the angels, and believed in the God who told him. This was not extraordinary in itself except in the consequences which arose from his jealous and sinful, faithless brother.

Noah believed what God had said and got on with his building. Surely, this is something we can imitate in our own lives.

Abraham left home when he was young, certainly in the first third of his life. Some of us have responded in our youth and we should encourage others too to take up the cross at a young, but responsible age.

Sarah believed what the Lord God had told her. She did no great thing beyond this in order to conceive.

Isaac's blessing of Jacob and Esau was under great stress when the Lord corrected his first intentions.

Moses' parents were faithful to Moses and to God when they hid him in faith.

There is nothing in the Joshua record about the faith which brought down the walls of Jericho, but it is there in the Hebrews record. Was this the faith of Joshua alone? The Joshua account does not say that Joshua passed on to the people what he had been promised about the walls.

Thus, in addition to the great things which great men and women did, there are the lesser and sometimes seemingly ordinary things which receive commendation from the Lord. May it not be that they did great things because they took the trouble to do the smaller things well and in faith?

These smaller things are by named and unnamed men and women, young and old, parents and others; at home and abroad, during the night or the day. Surely, there is encouragement for us in this wide range of examples and forerunners!

Lay aside every Weight

There is no way in which we can succeed if we are cumbered about with many unnecessary things. No one in a hurry deliberately picks up extra weight to carry. No runner develops more fat to his body. No one who swims puts lead weights on his ankles. This exhortation to "lay aside" is spiritual common sense. It is almost as if we threw off the trailing garment in the very act of getting on with the race.

The word is used in a variety of places and all with the same intent: "putting away all filthiness" (James 1:21, RV); "laying aside all malice and all guile" (1 Peter 2:1); "put away ... the old man" (Ephesians 4:22); "put away lying" (verse 25); "put ye also away all these: anger, wrath, malice ..." (Colossians 3:8, RV).

These are starkly wrong things (though we may possess them). There are others, too: unwise use of our time, self-indulgence, holidays away from places where ecclesias are to be found, encumbering our homes with expensive and beguiling time-wasters. You can think of your own temptations of various kinds.

But laying aside "every" weight is followed by "and" – an additional thing. It is something which no one escapes from easily: "the sin which doth so easily beset us."

"The sin" is not our particular "besetting" sin – which is the usual usage of this passage, as though we had a particular sin (which, doubtless, we have) to which attention is being directed. That is included, but the meaning is "sin itself" – the opposition to God.

Sin always tries to run away from God; it never contributes to the race. Sin always faces the other way; sin looks back to Babylon and not on to Zion.

Sin is native to us, at home with us, and "easily entangles" (NIV), or "clings so closely" (RSV); it is a competitor out to beat us, someone seeking to thwart our best plans. Sin has to be renounced.

The Way to Succeed

"Let us run". This is the first thing – we must run. We must determine to run. We have a goal, a target, an end; we have a purpose in life. We are not running anywhere and everywhere. We are running to Christ who is our life. Millions of men and women have no purpose, nowhere to go. We are blessed indeed.

Run "with patience". This is not the condition of quiet acceptance of the buffeting of life – "patience on a monument smiling at grief" – it is endurance and perseverance. This is 'stickability', not turning back, "not casting away your confidence which has great recompense of reward", "not drawing back unto perdition".

The race is "set before us". It lies before us (to the view); it is present (to the mind); it stands forth (as an example). The verb is translated "be first", in the expression, "if there be first a willing mind" (2 Corinthians 8:12). In the Septuagint it is translated "cleave". In other words, if we face the right way, the path is plain and we are on it. We have found it; we entered in by the narrow gate. The way was provided by God; we did not have to make it for ourselves – because we could not do so. The Way is Jesus Christ our Lord.

"Looking unto Jesus"

"We see Jesus crowned with glory and honour" was how this epistle set him forward at the beginning. It is not simply that we see him as an example; he has already arrived at the point for which we are making. He is he forerunner to eternal life.

"Fixing our gaze" on Jesus is the secret of success. As he set his gaze upon God – "I foresaw the Lord always before my face" (Acts 2:25, citing Psalm 16:8) – so we look upon him, and if so, then he will be at our right hand, as God was for Jesus.

Our Salvation

We look to Jesus as the "Author", meaning 'Captain' or 'Prince'. Liddell and Scott give as meanings: leader, founder, first father, prince, chief, first cause, author. It also occurs in:

"The captain of their salvation"   (Hebrews 2:10)

"Killed the Prince of life" (Acts 3:15)

" A Prince and a Saviour" (5:31)

He is not only the author, prince and leader – he is also the "finisher of our faith". "Finisher" means 'perfecter, the maker of the completion'. He is the author and perfecter of our faith. There is a process through which he went to do this:

"Make the captain of their salvation perfect through sufferings." (Hebrews 2:10)

"And having been made perfect (RV), he became the author of eternal salvation unto all them that obey him." (5:9)

This is he whom we remember. He set his attention on the joy before him and passed through the valley of tears and sorrow, enduring the cross; despising the shame, and is set down at the right hand of the throne of God.

15

"TIME WOULD FAIL ME ..."

10th June

Judges 7,8   **Isaiah 34**   **James 5**

THERE could not be a wider contrast than our three readings for today. Nor could there be a more pointed lesson that the whole of scripture is the only way in which to gain a balanced and proper perspective of all things spiritual.

Our readings in Judges take us back into a time of Israel's despair and the deliverance wrought by the Lord. The reading in Isaiah 34 speaks of the day when God will resolve the controversy of Zion, and heaven and earth, the present order of things, shall pass away as the Lord has said in the Olivet prophecy. And James provides his uncompromising approach to life in the Truth and at the same time exhorts us on the need to be ready for the coming of the Lord.

Isaiah 34 contains the words: "Seek ye out the book of the LORD, and read." This is the key to understanding and to stability in these last days. We live in a bewildering world when everything from BSE* (another of the pestilences of the last days) to the threatened break up of the USSR** cause the mind to stagger in seeking to grasp what is going on. God's answer is: "Seek ye out the book of the LORD, and read."

Why?

All of God's people come up against the whys of life. With the word of God on the one hand and the situation around us in our world and in our daily lives, we are constrained to ask, "Why?"

Look at Gideon in Judges 6. An angel of the Lord is delivering the word of God (verses 11-13). Sitting under the oak in Ophrah he meets Gideon the Abi-ezrite of the

---

* Bovine spongiform encephalopathy, commonly known as mad cow disease.

** Exhortation originally given in June, 1990.

tribe of Manasseh, who for fear of the Midianites is threshing his wheat in the winepress and not in some wide open space where the wind could blow away the chaff.

Gideon is called to service. He does not resist but has to cry out, "Why?" (verse 13). The Lord does not answer his question. When God calls there is no need for whys. Some brethren and sisters become discouraged about the world, the state of the brotherhood, family life and are reduced to despair and doubt by whys.

We have been called to service in the vineyard and ours is not to be hindered by whys but to get on with the work. Work for the Lord is the cure for evils and the best spiritual refresher available.

"The LORD is with thee"

"The LORD is with thee" was the message brought by the angel (verse 12) and repeated when Gideon felt unworthy for the task (verse 16): "Surely I will be with thee." They are words that go back to the beginning of things in God's dealings with the patriarchs, with Moses, with Joshua. It is a message for all of God's children: "Surely I will be with thee."

The Lord is Peace

Gideon was humble at heart and he had one 'why' which spoke well of him and made plain the grace of God. 'Lord, why have you chosen me?' The words were used by Moses and much later on by David. All of us from time to time in looking around have asked the same about ourselves: 'Why me?' The answer does not lie in us but in the wonderful mercy and grace of God. That is how He works; the reason lies in Him.

Gideon's response was to bring an offering to the Lord and to see whether it would be accepted. The angel waited whilst the offering was prepared. There is something very gracious about that. The "present", as the AV terms it, was accepted by fire from the altar of natural, unfashioned (by human hands) rock.

When assured by the Lord that the wondrous events did not betoken his death, Gideon prepared an altar for the Lord and gave it the name Jehovah-shalom, 'the LORD is peace'. This is one of a series of named altars. Abraham's altar was Jehovah-jireh, 'The LORD will provide' (Genesis 22:14); Jacob's was El-elohe-Israel, 'God, the God of Israel' (33:20) and El-beth-el (35:7), 'God of Bethel'. The wilderness altar, after the defeat of Amalek, had been Jehovah-nissi, 'The LORD is my banner' (Exodus 17:15). These speak a flowing message which runs through the emblems we share this morning.

Down with Baal and Astarte

An altar to the Lord was one thing, but how could it exist in the presence of the altar of Baal and the grove to the idol of Astarte? At the Lord's command, Gideon undertook a work of demolition at night and made a sacrifice on a new altar to the Lord lit by the wood of the Asherah.

This was a work of great courage and was Gideon's preparation for the defeat of the Midianites. It was a work he carried out by night. Doubtless the Lord would have preserved him had he gone about the task in daylight, but he was afraid and did the work at night. Sometimes in our lives we lack courage and still want to do the right thing. The Lord will accept us if we are seeking to be obedient to him. Moreover, Gideon's courage moved his father to defend him when the city was moved against his son. Faith is infectious.

Signs of Blessing

Gideon's fleece and the twofold answer from the Lord prepared the man for his task. The Lord was merciful and responded to his need and gave him answers without upbraiding His servant. There are those who have sought answers from the Lord in the same way; not miracles as such but answers to prayer in times of great difficulty in making decisions. God answers faithful prayer.

The Army is too Big

Gideon had sought to muster an army from Manasseh, Naphtali, Zebulun and Asher. 32,000 men responded and the Lord asked for the test laid down in Deuteronomy 20:8 to be applied. 22,000 men turned back because they had fearful hearts, but even the remaining 10,000 were too many and the Lord "tried" them (Judges 7:4). The word "tried" means 'refined'. The water test produced the required result. It is like the call to baptism which proves to be too much for some but purifying for others.

Three hundred men remained and the Midianites numbered 135,000 (8:10) – four hundred and fifty to one! All was now ready. The men were equipped with ram's horns, torches and earthenware pitchers. God gave Gideon and his armour bearer, Phurah, the sign of the loaf of barley bread tumbling, rolling, into the Midianite camp to destroy the tent of the king (7:13).

We, too, are similarly equipped. We have the torch of the Truth, but it is kept in an earthen vessel that the excellency of the power might be of God and not of ourselves. We have the ram's horn, the sounding Gospel to make known to others. This is equipment to work amongst the Midianites of our age.

The Sign of the Barley Loaf

And we have the sign of the barley loaf. It was the time of barley harvest when the Lord died. It was Passover time. The Lord is our Loaf, the sure sign that the Lord God is victorious and we can fight the good fight unafraid. We remember him this morning. We too are the loaf – we are one body, the faithful three hundred, refined and equipped for the war.

As with Gideon, so with us: "Surely the LORD is with thee."

16

SECRET STRENGTH
25th June

1 Samuel 4   **Isaiah 50**   Revelation 10,11

EVERY disciple wonders, when he contemplates Christ, how he endured such sufferings and contradiction of sinners against himself. Truly, he was a vessel specially prepared by the Father to accomplish what no other man could do; nevertheless, he shared our infirmities of the flesh and was tempted in all points like unto his brethren. How then, when it came to the final hours, did he bear himself with such grace and spiritual dignity in the face of unspeakable horrors and despicable ignominy and shame?

One of the Ways he endured

From time to time the scriptures open a window for us to see the Lord at work, not as a spectator looking at an outward scene, but as a privileged person gazing through a window into the mind of Christ. This is particularly true when the Lord is communing with his Father in prayer.

Look at Isaiah 50, one of our readings for today; have it open before you and look at Jesus. You will see him at work in a wondrous way. It is as though he is speaking quietly to himself and contemplating his work of redemption:

> "The Lord GOD hath given me the tongue of the learned, that I should know how to speak a word in season to him that is weary." (verse 4)

We are the weary ones; weary of our sins. Sometimes we are weary of the journey to the kingdom. Sometimes we are weary of the burdens we have to bear. The Lord wants to tell us a secret of endurance. Notice how he says that the Lord has given him the tongue of the learned. This does not mean an erudite, intellectual tongue. The RV says, "the tongue of them that are taught"; and the RV margin says, "the tongue of disciples". In other words,

Jesus knows how to speak to disciples because he is a disciple himself.

All of us know how much easier it is to learn from someone who has had precisely our experience. A young wife expecting her first baby likes to talk to someone who also has had a baby. A man who has lost his job likes to listen to someone who also has been made redundant. Such people speak to us from our side of the fence. They do not speak at us, they talk with us. The Lord Jesus is like that.

How did he learn to speak a word in season or as the NIV puts it, "to know the word that sustains the weary"? There were two ways: he had been weary himself and his Father had taught him because he was willing to learn. The rest of verse 4 is helpful:

"He wakeneth morning by morning, he wakeneth mine ear to hear as the learned [they that are taught, disciples]."

Whether or not the Father spoke directly to Jesus each morning we do not know. Certainly, there was a marvellous affinity between Father and Son. But any such communication is not open to disciples generally, and the morning by morning is explained by "as disciples".

What is it that each of us has and can make use of morning by morning? Two things above all else: prayer and the word of God. Our prayers pour out our praises and thankfulness, and express our needs to God. The word is God speaking to us. If we practise these blessings each day and throughout the day, our ear will be opened. We shall be instructed in the way that we should go. The word of God contains all the guidance we need, even in dire extremities.

If ye will receive it

The Bible tells us things we do not want to hear. It makes known our failings, offers guidance in making daily decisions and instructs us in godliness. Some of the lessons are painful because they run counter to our natural inclinations. Wise men listen: only fools believe they know better than God – "Fools hate knowledge"

(Proverbs 1:22). Therefore we must incline our ear to God if we want to endure unto salvation.

In Isaiah 50 we learn how Christ would speak when he came:

> "The Lord GOD hath opened mine ear, and I was not rebellious, neither turned away back."   (verse 5)

This is the window into the mind of Christ. He could have rebelled and turned back, his weak flesh would urge him so to do. Instead he listened, listened and listened to his Father until the Father's word became a part of his own will and wishes. The word "opened" means to open wide, not partially but altogether, as when one carves a slice of meat and totally exposes it. Another word for "opened" occurs in Psalm 40:6 where it means to pierce.

This latter word describes what a servant did who wished to remain in his master's service, even though the time for his release had come. His master bored through the lobe of his ear and this became a sign of perpetual and willing service – a free man willingly becoming a servant for life.

This is what God wishes us to become. His daily word is designed to help us to make that decision. If we pray and read with intent and dedication we shall find the same thing happening to us. There is no short cut, no instant obedience. Even of Christ it is written: "He learned obedience."

The Amazing Result

We asked how the Lord could achieve such composure and righteousness even when under great pain and provocation. We have been told how he did it. And the result?

> "I gave my back to the smiters, and my cheeks to them that plucked off the hair: I hid not my face from shame and spitting."   (Isaiah 50:6)

Not rebellious, not even simply passive, but altogether and completely making the Father's will his own for our sakes.

None of us can reach those heights of obedience, but we must seek to follow him. We now know the 'how' of the victory of Christ – his miraculous birth, his willing ear and his prayers, and the resultant strength to overcome.

Is the victory our own?

To ask the question is to answer it. God is our Father and He draws near to help us when we draw nigh to Him. Jesus would say:

> "For the Lord GOD will help me; therefore shall I not be confounded: therefore have I set my face like a flint, and I know that I shall not be ashamed. He is near that justifieth me; who will contend with me? let us stand together: who is mine adversary? let him come near to me. Behold, the Lord GOD will help me; who is he that shall condemn me?" (verses 7-9)

In ways beyond our understanding the Lord helps us. The repentant thief was near to Jesus as both of them were dying: the thief was blessed and Christ was comforted. It was all the work of the Father. And so there are circumstances in our own lives, though we cannot always see them, when our Father is specially at work. He supports and blesses us. This is our never-failing encouragement. Let us then take heart as we take bread and wine, and rejoice in the assurance meant for each of us – personally:

> "Who is among you that feareth the LORD, that obeyeth the voice of his servant, that walketh in darkness, and hath no light? let him trust in the name of the LORD, and stay upon his God." (verse 10)

17

DAVID AND GOLIATH
5th July

1 Samuel 17   Isaiah 61   Matthew 6

THE account in 1 Samuel 17 is amongst the best known in scripture whether among the young or the old. It never fails to stir and its simplicity is astonishing. The shepherd versus the man of war, the man of sin.

In one sense it is all larger than life, beyond the possible experience of any of us. David is a special person. In another sense there are basic principles at work that are common to all of us. What is written is for our benefit and example.

Preparation

"Then answered one of the servants, and said, Behold, I have seen a son of Jesse the Bethlehemite, that is cunning in playing, and a mighty valiant man, and a man of war, and prudent in matters, and a comely person, and the LORD is with him." (1 Samuel 16:18)

The shepherd used his time well, not idly dreaming his life away, but ranging beyond his sheep to music and intelligent meditation and understanding. Nevertheless, he cared for his charges and was obedient to his father, Jesse.

Whatever our daily occupation, God has given us a mind able at any time to think upon things eternal and, wherever we are, we can have His word to inform us. No one needs to be ignorant about life and its purposes, or about God and His ways. No one needs to be lonely: everyone can have the Lord with him. These are precious and very real things.

Hannah was a mother and a servant of the Lord God whose spirituality took her beyond that of Eli, God's High Priest.

David the shepherd, unbeknown to himself, was being prepared to be king. The Lord, who knows the end from the beginning, can, if we have faith in him, prepare us now for what lies ahead. There are no surprises for God.

Goliath the Champion

This man Goliath was a relic from the past. He was of the children of Anak whom the children of Israel had failed to annihilate. As with Israel, our past failures can overtake us in later life, unless we take the right steps to seek forgiveness and to overcome them.

Goliath, whose name means 'splendour', was just a great hulk of flesh. Saul and his men saw only Goliath, and not the Lord their God. God was smaller than Goliath in their eyes. Israel were the grasshoppers all over again and their enemies the giants.

This inversion is a common failing in personal and ecclesial life. With God, there are no problems, only answers – and we need to believe it. They may not be easy answers, but they will be answers, unless we make our God too small. Goliath was only sound and fury, and who was David to be afraid of a man who shall perish?

The word "champion" (in 17:4,23) means 'the man between the two camps', but in verse 51 it means 'mighty man, warrior'. Life consists of opposing forces, for and against the Truth, for and against eternal life. We need a man in between who can help us, one of us but mightier than we are, and such we have in the Lord Jesus Christ. He is the mediator between God and man. He is the slayer of the brazen Goliath, the opposer of the living God.

The Scene is set

Forty days of bellowing and boasting; forty days of fear and trembling. Where now were the 'head and shoulders' of king Saul, where were Abner and Joab? Perhaps it was David who made mighty men and not mighty men who made David. There are many who are valiant for Christ, because he has been valiant for them.

From the quiet keeping of the sheep there appeared a man in obedience to his father's will (verse 17), to look how his brethren fared (verse 18), who through fear of death were all their lifetime subject to bondage.

David was zealous for the name of his God and filled with disdain for the gods of the Philistines. The "living God" was his God, and the Philistine was a man of brass – sin incarnate.

David was isolated by incredulity and disbelief, as was his greater Son: "Neither did his brethren believe in him" (John 7:5). David relied on his faith in God. We have no knowledge that the Lord God had given him any charge, any revelation. It was simply the rightness of things that moved him.

David cared for God and for God's people. As a shepherd he had challenged a lion and a bear; Goliath was no different and by the eye of faith he saw him already dead.

David, too, would stand between the armies, not to indulge in empty boasting, but to defend the honour of his God.

Our sins find us out

The Philistines were already on the territory of Israel. Shochoh and Azekah were places in the inheritance of Judah, but the Philistines had been allowed to take them over.

It is so in life. We let God's territory pass into the hands of the enemy and sow the seeds of future threats and disasters. We let God's time be taken over by the media or by pleasure or by neglect. We let the safety of our family go by default because we fail to bring them up aright, and then complain that they are ill-behaved and undisciplined. The Philistines have to be challenged – the very word means 'migratory' or 'immigrants'. Philistines will always come into other people's land; and, of course, in the English language, to be a Philistine means to be a destroyer of culture.

We have to be strong and challenge those things and those people who stand where God should stand in our lives. In these days when the Philistines are everywhere, destroying marriages and the standards of marriage, replacing honesty with expediency and self, bringing covetousness instead of worship of God, we must make a stand. The Philistines teach in our schools, run the social sciences, wear the guise of sociologists, provide entertainment and ghetto-blast their way into our homes. David would have none of these things. David saw life clearly, more clearly than he sometimes saw it later on in the times of his troubles. He had no doubts that God would work and the old words "the LORD is with him", would be made plain. He knew that God had been with Joseph in the land of Egypt, with Jacob in Laban's land, with Moses in Midian, and he believed that God would be with him. He had no concern for himself, but rather for his God. God would take care of him.

There is a devastating simplicity about all of this. We make our lives too complicated and become weighed down by ifs and buts and maybes, or sap the positive goodness by wholesale and fruitless negatives. But our God is not an if, a but or a maybe; He is the Lord God Almighty as He had declared himself long ago to Jacob.

The Ravine

There was a deep ravine between Israel and the Philistines, so deep in fact that it is not visible until you are right near to it. Shouts carried across it, but to pass over it was needful to descend.*

It is like life. Sometimes to pass nearer to the kingdom we have to descend into the ravine: sorrows, trials, adversities or even the valley of the shadow of death. Life's giants look bigger for a while and tower above us, the floods seem to overwhelm us, but it is there that we find the smooth stones for our sling. Worn smooth by the water, they are ideal for their purpose.

"I will guide thee with mine eye", says the Lord. Adversity and God are an invincible combination. A good eye was useless without the sling and stone; a sling and stone would fail without a good eye; and sling and stone and eye would fail without the blessing of God.

The Septuagint expands the title of Psalm 144. The AV has "A Psalm of David" to which the Septuagint adds, "concerning Goliath". This is probably because of verse 3 which is common with verse 4 of Psalm 8. The

---

* C R Conder – Palestine Exploration Fund

subscription to Psalm 8, "upon Muth-labben" means 'relating to the death of the champion (Goliath)'.

"Blessed be the LORD my strength, which teacheth my hands to war, and my fingers to fight."

(Psalm 144:1)

So it is in life's battles. None is mightier than our God and His wisdom is profitable to direct.

The Weapons of our Warfare

David had said that he would cut off Goliath's head, but David had no sword! He would have to disarm the Philistine. He fully believed that he would. More particularly, he believed that God would and that is why he said:

"And all this assembly shall know that the LORD saveth not with sword and spear: for the battle is the LORD's, and he will give you into our hands."

(1 Samuel 17:47)

It is interesting that David had arrived at the battle-field when carrying out an entirely different mission. His father had sent him "to look how thy brethren fare" (verse 18). David's concern for them, and his father's concern for them, led him to this other and greater task which proved to be even better for his brethren's welfare than when he first arrived on the scene.

In undertaking the task he had his normal, daily accoutrement – a staff, a purse, a sling – the things with which he was familiar and had proved. We do not overcome our sudden problems by something new on the spot, but by what we have done with our characters in normal daily life. All of us are being saved by the Good Shepherd's equipment, the very things he used in his daily life.

Lessons for All

The incident – and it took time – made others think:

"Yet a man is risen to pursue thee, and to seek thy soul: but the soul of my lord shall be bound in the bundle of life with the LORD thy God; and the souls of thine enemies, them shall he sling out, as out of the middle of a sling." (1 Samuel 25:29)

"Persecutions, afflictions, which came unto me at Antioch, at Iconium, at Lystra; what persecutions I endured: but out of them all the Lord delivered me."
(2 Timothy 3:11)

"Save me from the lion's mouth: for thou hast heard me from the horns of the unicorns." (Psalm 22:21)

"I will praise thee, O LORD, with my whole heart; I will shew forth all thy marvellous works." (Psalm 9:1)

The Good Shepherd's Shepherd

"The LORD is my shepherd; I shall not want. He maketh me to lie down in green pastures: he leadeth me beside the still waters. He restoreth my soul: he leadeth me in the paths of righteousness for his name's sake. Yea, though I walk through the valley of the shadow of death, I will fear no evil: for thou art with me; thy rod and thy staff they comfort me. Thou preparest a table before me in the presence of mine enemies: thou anointest my head with oil; my cup runneth over. Surely goodness and mercy shall follow me all the days of my life: and I will dwell in the house of the LORD for ever." (Psalm 23:1-6)

18

"ALL THINGS WORK TOGETHER ..."
31st July

2 Samuel 17   **Jeremiah 21**   **Romans 7,8**

THIS is the end of Bible School week; the time for farewells and the time to head for home.* We have been welded together for a week with a common purpose around the word of God, in one life with a special routine, and with the world around us stopped short at the gates.

Now it will be different. The tide around us will come again bringing ordinary life, at work, at home, at college, and life's particular joys and sorrows. There is a feeling that life here and life there are two different things, as though we shifted from one set of clothes to another. If the two sets of life are different we have got to start making them the same. Life in Christ must be consistent wherever we lead it: if it isn't, then Christ is divided, and that cannot be right.

In our readings today we read:

"And we know that all things work together for good to them that love God, to them who are the called according to his purpose."   (Romans 8:28)

There is a converse to that verse, namely, all things do not work together for good to those who do not love God. If we exclude God from our daily lives – the normal life at home – by neglecting the word, allowing the media to take over, getting our priorities wrong, all things will go another way – *all* things, not simply some of them. If we have wrong friends, habitual bad behaviour, obsessions about business, double standards about our marriage, then *all* things will be wrong.

There are four people in today's readings where you will see that this is true, disastrously so for three of them.

* Given at Midwest Bible School (Hanover, Indiana, USA), July 1993.

They are Ahithophel, Abiathar and David in 2 Samuel 17, and Zedekiah in Jeremiah 21.

David and those about him

It is the time of Absalom's rebellion, and he is riding on the crest of the wave. He is ready to strike the death-blow upon David's reign. David is on the run, camped by the fords in the plains of Jericho, but, because he is a godly man, all things are working together for good. God is on his side.

Absalom has called together his advisers to discuss how to strike against David, and Ahithophel ('brother of folly') has been called in to give his counsel to the rebel 'king'. 'Strike now, right away', was his advice. His advice was probably good, but it came from a treacherous heart. He had thrown in his lot with the false Absalom and had forsaken David, to whom he had been both counsellor and friend:

"For it was not an enemy that reproached me; then I could have borne it: neither was it he that hated me that did magnify himself against me; then I would have hid myself from him: but it was thou, a man mine equal, my guide, and mine acquaintance. We took sweet counsel together, and walked unto the house of God in company." (Psalm 55:12-14)

Here was the forerunner of Judas and he comes to an identical end. Another psalm spoke of him in this way:

"Let their habitation be desolate; and let none dwell in their tents. For they persecute him whom thou hast smitten; and they talk to the grief of those whom thou hast wounded. Add iniquity unto their iniquity: and let them not come into thy righteousness. Let them be blotted out of the book of the living, and not be written with the righteous." (Psalm 69:25-28)

Ahithophel had reason to look upon David with some disfavour for he was Bathsheba's grandfather. But he looked on God's grace extended to the sinner David as being wrong, and thereby flew in the face of God, and all things worked together against him.

Not that God destined him for destruction regardless of his character, but because of his character. He had walked

98

with the righteous David, seen the word of the Lord at work in him and had chosen the path of the adversary, the adversary of the Lord's anointed. He fought against the Spirit of God, and was sure to lose.

The lessons are there for all of us: we can choose between seeking to please God or to please ourselves, to have all things working together for good, or working to our own destruction. There is no middle course.

It all worked out in a seemingly 'natural' way. Hushai's counsel prevailed:

> "The counsel that Ahithophel hath given is not good at this time (or, this time is not good, RV) ... for the LORD had appointed to defeat the good counsel of Ahithophel."
>
> (2 Samuel 17:7,14)

Hushai's counsel flattered Absalom, and at the same time contained the seeds of Absalom's own destruction: "Go to battle in thine own person."

Ahithophel's vanity was injured and, moreover, he knew that the rebellion was doomed to failure. He departed to wind up his earthly affairs with care and orderliness, and left his spiritual life in tatters.

Abiathar ('father of abundance')

There was another man whose life was at some point already faulty, but had not yet been revealed. You know how it can be? Abiathar was a descendant of Eli whose house was destined to be bereft of the high priesthood:

> "Wherefore the LORD God of Israel saith, I said indeed that thy house, and the house of thy father, should walk before me for ever: but now the LORD saith, Be it far from me; for them that honour me I will honour, and they that despise me shall be lightly esteemed. Behold, the days come, that I will cut off thine arm, and the arm of thy father's house, that there shall not be an old man in thine house. And thou shalt see an enemy in my habitation, in all the wealth which God shall give Israel: and there shall not be an old man in thine house for ever. And the man of thine, whom I shall not cut off from mine altar, shall be to consume thine eyes, and to grieve thine heart: and all the

99

increase of thine house shall die in the flower of their age." (1 Samuel 2:30-33) This did not mean that Abiathar was thereby condemned or that he was not allowed to serve the Lord. It was Abiathar who determined that. For whatever reason (2 Samuel 8) it was clear to David that Zadok was to be given preferential treatment by his attending the tabernacle for the Ark in Jerusalem, whist Abiathar remained at Gibeon with the altar and the tabernacle made by Moses.

When Adonijah sought to usurp the rights of king Solomon, Abiathar threw in his lot with him and thereby was excluded from the priesthood. A serious, uncorrected fault in our life destroys the whole of life – it destroys all things.

Zedekiah

This man, whose name means 'Jah is might or right'; or 'Jah is righteous', illustrates the choice which lies before all of us. He had access to direct counsel from Jeremiah which gave clear warning and good promises if the king obeyed. Moreover, in his heart, the king knew that Jeremiah was good and true and righteous, and that the word of God spake through him. But he refused it because he preferred his kingship and was afraid of his princes, counsellors and priests.

Even when, as Jeremiah had warned, Nebuchadnezzar commenced the siege, Zedekiah shut his eyes and his heart to truth as reiterated by Jeremiah. Right to the last – for the siege lasted almost two-and-a-half years – he persisted in folly and even sought to escape the word of God by fleeing from Jerusalem by night. He was overtaken by the Chaldean army by Jordan, in "the plains of Jericho", seemingly the very place where Israel kept the Passover at Gilgal when they first entered the Land.

At Riblah, Nebuchadnezzar slew Zedekiah's sons as Zedekiah stood by in chains, then thrust out his eyes before leading him blind to Babylon, the place to which he had been walking all his life (2 Kings 25 and Jeremiah 39). The fatal flaw in his character, a lover of men more than a lover of God and His word, meant that all things were wrong. It was Zedekiah and not God who chose that destiny.

And what are the lessons for us? Here are four different men whose fate was sealed, not by capricious predestination, but by their own choices, the very choices of their hearts.

All of them sinned. It was not sin that barred the way for Ahithophel, Abiathar and Zedekiah, but unforgiven sin – the sin that marked their way of life, their personal choice of sin as the thing preferred.

The lesson is clear. We have been called and given an undeniable hope. Let us hold to it at home, at work, at college, always:

"And we know that all things work together for good to them that love God, to them who are the called according to his purpose."   (Romans 8:28)

19

PROVED BY HARD QUESTIONS
15th August

1 Kings 10   **Jeremiah 36**   **Mark 10**

LIFE has many hard questions, some beyond our understanding, and others where the answer is as hard as the question. Question and answer is one of the most effective ways of teaching and of learning. Children love to be tested, and later on, when in their teenage years, they switch roles and become the question master.

Sometimes the questions are spoken and sometimes implied, as we shall discover in our readings today.

The Challenge of Jeremiah

It is a strange feature of human nature that it will embrace folly even when the plain facts of the case are well known. Take, for example, Jehoiakim who features in our reading from Jeremiah. The prophet had repeatedly sounded warnings about the fall of Jerusalem. In fact, Nebuchadnezzar had already left Babylon on a mission by which he was to inflict damage on all the kingdoms in his path, and right down to Egypt.

Nevertheless, Jeremiah had been put under some kind of restraint (36:5) and the king and the princes were implacably set against him.

Baruch's background is one of being brother to the man who in due course would be Zedekiah's chief chamberlain. But he was Jeremiah's faithful amanuensis and accurately took down what Jeremiah dictated to him. Then, at some risk in due course to himself, he goes first to the chamber of Gemariah the son of Shaphan, where he reads the word of God through Jeremiah to all the people. What he read was known to Micaiah, Gemariah's son, who, perceiving the seriousness of the message, told the princes. Baruch is then led to read the message again, this time to all the princes and to other men of standing, these latter including some who were committed to the word of God.

103

The princes caused Baruch to tell them how he had written down the words. He told them. They took the roll and instructed Baruch to go into hiding with Jeremiah. They went to the king where Jehudi, who had taken the scroll from Elishama, read Jeremiah's message to the king who featured in the denunciations.

As the roll was read, the king cut away the columns and burned them in the brazier in the winter house where he was, until the whole of the roll had been consumed by the flames.

Thus a fool and a defier of the Lord God thought to nullify His word and the threatened consequences. He was later to be given the burial of an ass and cast out of Jerusalem.

The Word Today

We, too, have had the word read to us with its solemn exhortations from the Lord himself. None of us is likely to follow Jehoiakim in his folly. Our risk is always one of neglect by which the columns of scripture are cut out of our lives because we do not read and take heed. If we were to persist in such a course, we too would be barred from Jerusalem when the king comes.

There were men in today's chapter whose reverence for God and His word is undoubted. The family of Shaphan is a case in point. One of them, Shaphan's son Ahikam, hid Jeremiah from harm in the first year of Jehoiakim's reign (26:24). Another, Shaphan's grandson Michaiah, took heed of the word he heard and warned others as recorded in verse 13 of today's chapter. So, as in our own time, there were those who took heed and believed. They gave more than a cup of cold water to the prophet and will be rewarded accordingly.

We need to have a chamber (verse 10), like that of Gemariah, Shaphan's son – a place in our hearts for Jeremiah where his word can be read in quietness and humbly believed and acted upon.

Journey to Jerusalem

In Mark 10 the Lord is on his last journey to Jerusalem. Having left Capernaum, he is travelling on the far side, the east side, of Jordan. The question which exercised him, having been put by the Pharisees, was one which concerns us in these days: divorce and remarriage.

This not the time to discuss the implications of this issue, but we need to take note of the remarks of Jesus in response to the problems of his own time. Divorce came about by the "hardness of your hearts". In other words, there had entered into marriage from one side or the other, or perhaps from both, that which is destructive of marriage – a hard, insensitive, self-centred heart.

All of us need to take note. If we wish to preserve our marriages, our hearts must be understanding one of another and caring for one another; caring for the other more than we care for ourselves.

The question that had been asked is one we met in the readings a week ago: Is it lawful?

"And it came to pass, that he went through the corn fields on the sabbath day; and his disciples began, as they went, to pluck the ears of corn. And the Pharisees said unto him, Behold, why do they on the sabbath day that which is not lawful?" (Mark 2:23,24)

Marriage has laws which govern it, but marriage does not thrive and become strong by law. It is when marriages break up that the law takes over. We are not to occupy our minds with what is lawful and what is not, otherwise we shall find ourselves in borderline disputes of the kinds that occupied the Jews. We need to work on the basis of grace – the compassionate, forgiving, enlarging and long-suffering virtue which goes beyond the second mile and never complains about it, but is glad for our partner's sake.

We shall not enter the kingdom of God by law. If the question at the gates of the kingdom were: Is it lawful to let them in? the answer would be, No. May I let them in by grace and compassion? Yes, if we are people of faith seeking to do His will.

Little Children

It cannot be coincidence that the very next incident, after the discussion about divorce, involves little children. The defenceless, the totally dependent, become the centre of the circle. Even the disciples tried to prevent the children being brought to Jesus in the mistaken view that Jesus was too busy.

We live in a world where people are too busy for children. The children are left to amuse themselves and to make their own choices. They are exposed to the world's influences without full parental guidance and not included in the proper family circle whereby the word of God and its outworking are clearly made known.

Jesus took them into his arms and blessed them. These were little children; "babes" is how they are described in Luke (18:15, RV). The greatest security we can offer our children lies in our willing love and in bringing them along the path that leads to Jesus Christ. It is little use concentrating on their secular education and employment, if we neglect the major privilege that is ours, namely, to offer them eternal life.

Never again in all their lives will the children have the kind of mind described by Jesus in the phrase, "receive the kingdom of God as a little child". Later on their minds will have been polluted and become more sophisticated. At the right age, they are wonderfully teachable, humbly and willingly learning.

If the Lord was indignant when children were barred from coming to him, is he likely to be less so if we are the barriers between our children and the way of life in him?

What shall I do?

This is the perennial question. It is life's question that arises time and again. In this case, the man was a ruler, a lawyer, and rich. But he was thoughtful about the future, about eternal life. Perhaps because of his background he thought in terms of doing one great thing. Would that it were so simple!

It is possible to think that the Lord told him to do one thing to ensure eternal life – selling all that he had. But that is not what the record says: "Sell whatsoever thou hast, and give to the poor ... and come, take up the cross, and follow me" (Mark 10:21). The answer is more complex than it appears at first. Indeed, the part that mattered in the end was to take up the cross and follow the Lord.

106

His riches were the barrier. It is true for all of us. There are things we are not willing to let go. These are our riches, whatever they are, and they vary from person to person. It was his riches that made him ask: "What shall I do?" He was not satisfied within himself, and sought a remedy. Jesus gave him the remedy. The remedy lay not in things, but in: "My son, give me thine heart" ... "for where your heart is, there will your treasure be also".

Children

The young ruler departing in sadness – 'lowring' is the word – and the words of Jesus, "How hardly shall they that have riches enter into the kingdom of God", created a problem for the disciples. They wanted to know "Who then can be saved?", and the Lord spoke to them. He addressed them as children, a link with the earlier incident, though a different word is used.

The young man's trust was in the wrong place. Shifting one's trust is not an easy thing. It creates uncertainty or, if we look at it the right way, it takes faith. To the disciples it seemed to be 'a hard thing'. There are no hard things for God. As He said at another time, "If it be marvellous in (your) eyes ... should it also be marvellous in mine eyes?" (Zechariah 8:6). That which is impossible with men, is possible with God. Indeed, the Lord pleads on that basis in Gethsemane: "All things are possible unto thee ..."

The young man had come, kneeling, and Jesus loved him. Perhaps, at a later time, he turned and humbling himself like a child, followed in the footsteps of Jesus. Many of our complications arise because we are juggling with too many things when just "one thing is needful".

Up to Jerusalem

"And they were in the way going up to Jerusalem; and Jesus went before them: and they were amazed; and as they followed, they were afraid. And he took again the twelve, and began to tell them what things should happen unto him." (Mark 10:32)

Notice how this incident is described: "they were in the way going up to Jerusalem". Here is more than a mere topographical allusion: it was the whole purpose of God in Christ.

107

They were amazed and afraid. What was it that set them in this frame of mind? Surely, it was something about the resolute face of Christ. More than that, he was the shepherd who was going before them. He had to lead them through the valley of the shadow of death. They were all unseeing and unknowing of the things that awaited them in the holy city.

Often in our daily lives we too are in ignorance of that which lies ahead. But he will never leave us or forsake us: he will always go before us. Time and again we are led to exclaim, "Surely, the LORD is in this place; and I knew it not".

The city knew not the time of her visitation and the things that belonged to her peace. But it was those things that the Lord would accomplish for his chosen. Calvary would demonstrate beyond all doubt the things that belong to our peace.

James and John

Salome had an intense interest in the eternal welfare of her children. Her faith in the kingdom was rock hard and she wanted them to have places of honour with Jesus. James and John went along with her wishes. They had the same deep faith in Christ as the King. Their request is interesting:

> "They said unto him, Grant unto us that we may sit, one on thy right hand, and the other on thy left hand, in thy glory." (Mark 10:37)

Christ did not rebuke but led them another way, much as a parent might do with his children. "Can you drink? ... ye shall indeed." "We must through much tribulation enter into the kingdom of God" (Acts 14:22).

Even so, the places on the right and on the left had already been prepared by God – and Jesus knew who would occupy them but did not divulge who it would be. We automatically think of noble characters: the fathers, David, and so it might be. But it may well be that the places will be taken by some unknown persons – unknown to us but beloved of the Father.

When they reached Jerusalem, they would learn a dreadful lesson. The places on the right and the left were taken by two thieves – also "prepared of my Father". And one of them would use words of similar import to those of James and John: "Remember me when thou comest into thy kingdom."

A Blind Beggar by the Highway

In Mark 10, the Lord declares: "For even the Son of man came not to be ministered unto, but to minister, and to give his life a ransom for many" (verse 45). Then, as Jesus and his disciples left Jericho, they were met by Blind Bartimaeus, who called out, "Jesus, thou Son of David, have mercy on me" (verses 47,48).

The juxtaposition of these two thoughts cannot be accidental. Bartimaeus is like all of us. Crying out for mercy, he is heard. Casting aside his garment, he sprang up. Then, so different from the young man who had asked, "What shall I do?" came the words: "What wilt thou that I should do unto thee?" And, seeing, he "followed Jesus in the way".

Blessed are these

In our first reading there is another individual who travelled to Jerusalem with hard questions. They were all answered, as ours can be, by standing before the Lord, and hearing his wisdom.

Like the Queen of Sheba, we can approach before the King. We gather at his table, which is royally prepared with the best food. He gave his body, his life-blood, himself, for the salvation of his people – not only to answer their hard questions, but to destroy the power of sin and open up a way to his Father and to life everlasting.

"And when the queen of Sheba had seen all Solomon's wisdom, and the house that he had built, and the meat of his table, and the sitting of his servants, and the attendance of his ministers, and their apparel, and his cupbearers, and his ascent by which he went up unto the house of the LORD; there was no more spirit in her. And she said to the king, It was a true report that I heard in mine own land of thy acts and of thy wisdom. Howbeit I believed not the words, until I came, and mine eyes had seen it: and, behold, the half was not told me: thy wisdom and prosperity exceedeth the fame which I heard. Happy are thy men, happy are these thy servants, which stand continually before thee, and that hear thy wisdom." (1 Kings 10:4-8)

20

BEFORE PASSOVER
19th August

1 Kings 14   Jeremiah 40   **Mark 14**

THE Passover meal was followed by seven days of unleavened bread. Of course there was no leaven in the house when the Passover was killed and the lamb was eaten with bitter herbs and unleavened bread. The priests and scribes were scheming to put Christ to death whilst Jesus was preparing for his sacrifice. The one preparation was evil and the other was the perfection of righteousness.

The apostles were unaware that the Lord was to die an atoning death. But someone had at least a premonition of that terrible event. She came with an alabaster cruse of pure nard, very precious, which she broke so that the ointment ran over the head of Jesus. "She is come aforehand to anoint my body to the burying". Why she should have anointed the body now and not as part of the ceremony in caring for the dead we do not know. There was an urgency in her mind – her gift was very precious. It is interesting that the word spikenard is at root associated with faith and assurance.

This loving deed was never to be forgotten and would be known all over the world wherever the Gospel was preached. The record in John tells us that the odour of the ointment filled the house, and it still does.

Jesus said two more words about this loving act. The first is very simple: "She hath done what she could." This is what the Lord requires of us – to do what we can and not what we cannot. Every opportunity to do what we can should be spurred by love for the Master. Secondly, it is recorded and read everywhere "for a memorial of her".

Moreover this deed was done in the house of a leper – whether cured or the disease was spent we do not know. If we do what we can in love for our Lord, it will be remembered.

111

The incident was marred by the hypocritical care for the poor by Judas. It cannot be a coincidence that the man who called this overflowing love purposeless waste is himself remembered by the Lord when he prays, saying that he has lost none of the apostles save this "son of perdition", this son of waste (John 17:12). Let not the overflowing love of Christ be wasted on us, rather let us keep the feast of memorial in sincerity and truth.

The 'Keeping' of the Passover

Where shall we keep the passover? Was this supper the actual Passover supper? If so, it would seem to contradict the words of Jesus: "With desire I have desired to eat this passover with you before I suffer." Therefore, the supper they held that night was not the one where the lamb was eaten.

What was it then? It was a preparatory supper ordained by Jesus. Interestingly, it was eaten on the day when the Lord would be crucified (twenty-four hours from 6 o'clock in the evening).

The word used for the venue – "guestchamber" (Mark 14:14) – is most interesting. The word for "inn" in the expression, "no room ... in the inn" (Luke 2:7) is precisely the same word as "guestchamber". Man had no room for Jesus in the inn but he has room for us in his guestchamber – "a large upper room". There is room for all who will come on the living way. This being so, we must show the same kind of magnanimity and generosity in our dealings with others.

Gethsemane

The place of the olive press was the place of excruciating prayer. Jesus led eight of the twelve disciples to one place apart and took the remaining three to another whilst he went to pray still further in the garden. He began to be sore amazed (the root means 'utterly astonished') and very heavy. A burden of unspeakable weight was coming to rest on his shoulders when the Lord would lay on him the iniquity of us all. It was beyond his strength to carry the load unaided. Gethsemane was the moment of truth, the time of resolution.

The three hour trial unfolded in a place which the twelve were accustomed to visit (like David with Olivet). Prayer is not something for special occasions; it is not the spare wheel – it is the steering wheel. Gethsemane would never have taken place successfully had not the Lord been often to the Father in prayer. He knew that this moment would come and, although he could not anticipate it by forestalling it, the Lord had already wrestled with the will of man in order to fulfil the will of God.

The last supper was passed and they had made their journey down the steps (traces of them remain to this day) and over the brook Kidron and entered the enclosed piece of ground known as the Garden of Gethsemane. It was full moon and the place would be one of light and shade.

The eleven were warned that prayer was the only way to victory over temptation and Peter had been warned against his 'cocksureness' – does this occasion provide the origin of the word? However, they were very weary from the long day and the strangeness of the day and the demeanour of their Lord. Perhaps, too, Judas' departure was affecting them. Two of them had swords.

The Lord followed his own advice and engaged in earnest prayer, the need for which arose from his mission that was unique to him and altogether essential for our salvation. The Lord knew of the demands on him and of his inner humanity which would seek to find another way. The Lord knew no other way, but wondered whether the Father in His inscrutable wisdom could provide such a way. The words he used are recorded for us in Mark:

> "Abba, Father, all things are possible unto thee; take away this cup from me: nevertheless not what I will, but what thou wilt." (14:36)

"Abba" is Aramaic for father, perhaps the actual word used by Jesus at home. I am uncertain (and the concordances do not admit it) about making the word to mean, papa, etc.. Abba occurs twice more in the New Testament: Romans 8:15 in connection with adopted children of God; Galatians 4:6 again in connection with children and in an obvious reference to Mark 14. In his agony, the Lord must have found the word reverently warm and right.

113

It is interesting that the expression "with God nothing shall be impossible" was used by Gabriel when he told Mary that she was to have a child though she was unmarried. The AV/RV margin says this is a citation from Genesis 18:14 (Greek), when the angel was making known to Sarah, who was barren, that she was to have a son. Mary must have often repeated to Jesus what the angel had said to her. The expression is used by God about Christ's work and similarly in His promise to Jeremiah that he would receive his inheritance in Anathoth despite the fact that the Chaldeans were besieging the city.

Surely, the Lord was not seeking to escape from the mission given to him by God and to which he had made reference on more than one occasion. He was seeking easement from the agony of the battle which he had faithfully joined. It was at this juncture that an angel appeared and strengthened him. With what words the angel did this merciful work we do not know. We, too, can pray for help in the difficult circumstances of life – sickness, temptation, bereavement for example.

The disciples had fallen asleep and must have looked shamefaced when the Lord wakened them, especially Peter: "Simon, sleepest thou? couldest not thou watch one hour?" – a sure reminder of what he had promised and a warning not to be self-reliant.

The Lord returned to his post of prayer. He went into a prayer that cannot be described in words but which caused him to perspire great drops as of blood falling to the ground. "In the sweat of thy face shalt thou eat bread" was the wording of the Edenic curse, but for us it means that there would have been no bread for this service except by the shocking agony of that hour.

Christ returned to the eleven and they were "sleeping for sorrow". The nature of their sorrow we can but surmise. There was bewilderment, for the heaviness of Christ was beyond them, even though they wished to help. But instead of persisting in prayer, the physical weakness of their flesh took them into deep sleep, as when a child cries himself to sleep.

"Except I drink it" was now the purpose of Christ without other words. Another hour of prayer completed the task. He was not simply repeating over and over again like a mantra a few hopeless words. He was seeking for strength and resolve. They came, wonderfully. He returned to the eleven and left them sleeping until he roused them to tell them that, in effect at that instant, the traitor was at work. The mob with torches, swords, sticks and other tools were descending into the heart of the garden and met Jesus face to face. This was not the Jesus who came into the garden three hours ago, heavy and in deep amazement. The battle was over and he had won.

The leaders of the mob were stricken to silence by the appearance of Christ. Perhaps they had expected that he would cringe before them, beseech them in some way or, perhaps, smite them by miracle. Instead they faced a man totally at peace with himself and his God, almost regal in his bearing and totally in control of the moment. His question, "Whom seek ye?" was powerful beyond words and they fell backwards to the ground, rose again to meet the same question and hear the same answer, "I am he".

Judas stepped forward and greeted the Lord with profuse kisses on his cheek. The Lord's response would burn in his heart until when, later in the day, he hanged himself. "Judas, betrayest thou the Son of man with a kiss?" Sin turns the simple, meaningful things of life into something hideous and revolting. Judas had had the opportunity to repent but his heart was set on evil and there was no way back for him.

Meanwhile, Peter's trial lay ahead. Faithfully he followed John to the palace of the high priest. Whilst the trial was going on, he was tempted by threatening questions, two from a maid. He had no strength and shivered in the cold until the cock crowed. Worse still, the Lord turned and looked on Peter and his whole world collapsed on him and he went into the darkness with bitter tears. There was a way back, as there is from all sin, but the upward way was initiated by the very Lord whom he had denied.

We are present in this solemn day in one or more of the characters portrayed for us. We need to take the lessons and turn again to the Lord to see him, to seek him and to remember him – and he will remember us.

21

THE BIRTH OF JESUS CHRIST
10th September

2 Kings 16   Ezekiel 6   **Luke 2**

THE seeming narrative record is in fact a basic teaching mechanism by which we learn about the nature of the Lord Jesus, his mission and our relationship to him. Obvious lessons are often passed by because the record of the event is so absorbing. Luke 2 is a model chapter for the true Bible student where care in reading and an awareness of the purpose of God serve to bring out the instruction we are intended to take

Six months before the time of the events of Luke 2, another child had been born – the forerunner, John the Baptist – who went before Christ in time but behind him in service.

The Enrolment

God who rules in the kingdom of men moved Caesar Augustus to order a taxing (an enrolment – a writing, by implication an assessment, a taxing). The mother-to-be was in Nazareth but Micah had foretold the birth as taking place in Bethlehem. This was David's city and Joseph was of the house and lineage of David; and so was Mary because Romans 1:3 tells us: "His Son Jesus Christ our Lord, which was made of the seed of David according to the flesh."

Thus, the Lord God brought His Son safely into the world in David's city. Great David's greater son, David's lord, came humbly into existence and was laid in a manger, a crib for animals' fodder. He who was to have dominion over all things came to the place where animals came; he who was to have dominion over them. Here in the lowliest of circumstances was Mary's firstborn and the Lord God's firstborn and only begotten Son.

Doubtless, Christ too was enrolled. He was numbered among the transgressors. "Of whom do the kings of the earth take custom or tribute? of their own children, or of

117

strangers?" (Matthew 17:25). Christ was a stranger and a pilgrim on earth. Even when he comes again, "the kings of the earth ... (will) take counsel together, against the LORD and against his anointed" (Psalm 2:2).

The Shepherds

The shepherds were the watchmen of the night ('keeping night-watches', RV margin). The watchmen on the hills were where David kept his sheep; where, perhaps, he composed the inspired words, "The Lord is my shepherd". Certainly, it was of those days that David was thinking when he penned the Psalm under God's hand. The shepherds typified the faithful in Israel who were waiting for the Messiah and of whom it was said: "The people were in expectation, and all men mused (reasoned) in their hearts of John, whether he were the Christ or not" (Luke 3:15).

The picture of sheep and their shepherd was the constant preoccupation of the Lord Jesus Christ. We should therefore perhaps not be surprised that it was to shepherds that the revelation was made. "An angel of the Lord stood by them" (RV) and "the glory of the Lord shone round about them" (they were caught up in the shekinah glory).

The message "Good tidings of great joy" (Luke 2:10) proclaimed the Gospel in brief, the Gospel which ultimately was "to all the people", but to Israel in the first place.

All the names come together: "Saviour" (Jesus), and "Christ the Lord" (verse 11). Christ was born as Jesus, born as Christ and born as Lord ("the mother of my lord is come to me"). The sign was the swaddling, the swathing in strips of cloth, the garment of the poor. How strange that the clothing of his birth and of his death should be described for us!

Heaven's host sang their song of joy: "Glory to God in the highest" (verse 14) – the great prerequisite; that which will finally bring the blessings of the kingdom when all the earth shall be filled with God's glory.

And "On earth peace" – peace that was embodied at that moment in Christ's coming, and is revealed in Christ as "our peace", and later as "the Prince of peace".

"Among men in whom he is well pleased" (verse 14, RV): 'well pleased' is the word to be used later of the Lord Jesus himself and is here associated with the redeemed in anticipation of the redemptive work of Christ Jesus.

The shepherds' worship at the manger made the message known to Mary and Joseph, and published abroad the great news for the world.

Mary's Meditations

Mary could not have come even thus far without having been infinitely alone in her thinking. She was unique in the conception and the child she carried and bore. No one had ever had her experience. As it would be with her son later on, so now it was for Mary, there was no one on earth she could turn to in a common experience. This was not simply the birth of a child, wonderful as that is; it was the birth of God's Son.

She had "cast in her mind what manner of salutation this should be" when the news of her selection was made known by the angel Gabriel; now the message is opened even further by the revelation to the shepherds; and soon she would hear Simeon tell her of the destiny of Christ and of "a sword that shall pierce through thy own soul also" (verse 35).

Her feelings as a natural mother were possessed by this other-worldliness, the work of the Seed of the woman.

Cleansing

Christ was born under the law (Galatians 4:4) and he was of the seed of Abraham. On the eighth day he was circumcised. There would be another circumcision when he would be cut off from the land of the living – the circumcision of Christ.

Like unto his brethren

Christ was born of our very nature: "in all things it behoved him to be made like unto his brethren" (Hebrews 2:17). And, nowhere is this made plainer than in Mary's purification according to the Law (Leviticus 12:6-8). Unlike the Romish doctrine of an immaculate conception

119

of Mary and therefore of Christ, she was in all points like unto any other mother in Israel.

She brought her firstborn according to the Law. Every firstborn had to be redeemed by the payment of five shekels of the sanctuary (Numbers 18:15,16). "That take, and ... give for me and thee" was what Christ said about the piece of money, the shekel, found by Peter in the fish's mouth. Christ too shared redemption from death, sinless as he was.

Simeon and Anna

The old man, Simeon, was waiting for the Messiah, waiting for the consolation of Israel, and waiting in the temple. The Holy Spirit came upon him, first in revelation and then in guidance to bring him to the temple on the day of Mary's arrival with Jesus, "the Lord's Christ" (as at the transfiguration – 9:20).

He takes up the child: the old world with the new in his arms, and he prays for death. To see the child, the babe, was enough. He believed and in wonder declared: "Mine eyes have seen thy salvation" (Luke 2:30).

"The LORD hath made bare his holy arm in the eyes of all the nations; and all the ends of the earth shall see the salvation of our God." (Isaiah 52:10)

That salvation is embodied in Christ, first "to lighten the Gentiles" and then "the glory of thy people Israel" (Luke 2:32).

Mother and child were blessed of Simeon – the child as foretold by Isaiah:

"And he shall be for a sanctuary; but for a stone of stumbling and for a rock of offence to both the houses of Israel, for a gin and a snare to the inhabitants of Jerusalem." (8:14)

But for Mary there came the unexpected, the sudden fear and profound sorrow: "a sword shall pierce through thy own soul also." The death of Christ would bring this upon her. But, since "the thoughts of many hearts" were to "be revealed", the expression probably has reference also to the searching word of God:

"The word of God is quick, and powerful, and sharper than any two-edged sword, piercing even to the dividing asunder of soul an spirit, and of the joints and marrow, and is a discerner of the thoughts and intents of the heart." (Hebrews 4:12)

Anna (Grace) the prophetess is like the aged Eve, waiting. She is waiting for the redemption in (or, of) Jerusalem. She is the daughter of Phanuel – the face of God, and is of the tribe of Asher – happy, blessed. She now praises God for the one who would reveal the glory of God in his own face.

The Christ

The child was "filled with wisdom" (Luke 2:40), but not all at once as though he had everything from birth, for he "increased in wisdom and stature, and in favour with God and man" (verse 52).

Sat at home he would be subject to his parents even though he was beginning to outstrip them in understanding the word of God (verses 50,51).

The Passover

At the age of 12 (when Jewish boys became *bene hatorah* – sons of the Law), Jesus came to Jerusalem for the Passover which was the habit of his parents. It would also be Passover time at the end of his life and there would be another Joseph to take care of him. This time he is to be lost for three days, much as he would be 'lost' at the end of his life.

He who was the Lamb of God is found first active around the word of God, sitting among the doctors of the Law, "Hearing them, and asking them questions" (verse 46). Whilst his parents chide him for being lost, he replies saying to those who had said, "Thy father and I have sought thee sorrowing", "Wist ye not that I must be about my Father's business (in my Father's house, RV)" – a reply which left them puzzled and failing to understand.

The Passover had double meaning. At his birth there had been "no room for them in the inn". At the end he would assemble with his disciples "in a large upper room" (a "guestchamber" – same word as "inn"). So we assemble in 'the House of Bread' – Bethlehem – to keep the Passover of the Son of God.

COMFORT OF THE SCRIPTURES

22

THE UNJUST JUDGE
25th September

1 Chronicles 8   Ezekiel 21   **Luke 18**

THE setting of the parable is the Second Coming as in Luke chapter 17. This is the decisive day when some will be saved and many lost. The Lord wants us to be among the saved – and so do we. But we must really want to be saved, not by generalities but by diligent application. Salvation must be sought in earnest.

Prayer wins through

There is power in prayer; there is power in praying, for: "Men ought always to pray, and not to faint" (Luke 18:1). We are urged elsewhere to pray without ceasing, to pray always, and the lessons in those places are plain enough. Here it is different because we have alternatives set before us: praying and fainting. Prayerless men will faint in adversity; the Lord says so. Prayerful men and women will endure however hard the way – even though they may be defenceless, unrepresented widow women with the scales of consolation heavily loaded against them, as in this parable.

If we are becoming discouraged, if we sometimes wonder whether it is all worthwhile, if we sometimes despair of parts of our community or our ecclesia or our family, if we despair of ourselves, the answer is clear – pray, pray, pray. We must remember that at the other end of the line are two persons for whom discouragement does not exist, the Father and the Son.

God is never surprised or discouraged. His purpose will succeed. Christ is Victory enthroned with the Father. There is our guarantee. Things may appear to be different, but we must not judge by appearances or from a merely personal point of view. That is what the unjust judge was to do. So stand next to Christ and hear him say: "The Lord is on my side."

123

"I called upon the LORD in distress: the LORD answered me, and set me in a large place. The LORD is on my side; I will not fear: what can man do unto me?" (Psalm 118:5,6)

It is not unusual to feel that we are overwhelmed, as though the storm is bigger than our God. Others have felt the same way. It is our perspective which makes it seem that way:

"Fear not, Daniel: for from the first day that thou didst set thine heart to understand, and to chasten thyself before thy God, thy words were heard, and I am come for thy words. But the prince of the kingdom of Persia withstood me one and twenty days: but, lo, Michael, one of the chief princes, came to help me; and I remained there with the kings of Persia. Now I am come to make thee understand ..." (Daniel 10:12-14)

There are clear lessons for us from this. God hears faithful prayer right away. Seeming delay is not delay in hearing. God has a purpose into which our prayer fits. It is not that God had need of an angel to answer Daniel, there are thousands of them. It was that what Daniel requested was granted in the context of God's ongoing purpose of which Daniel was a beloved part. It was part of Daniel's education to see where he fitted, and it was a great consolation that although there were things which had to do with kings and kingdoms, Daniel was not forgotten at any time. In fact, it was on his and the saints' behalf that the purpose was being performed according to God's good and righteous pleasure.

Jeremiah had the same problem. As the Lord's faithful prophet, it seemed to him that it was he and not the wicked people who were suffering. But there was a right time for everything. The great nations were being moved, the wheel of history was turning; nevertheless, the Lord was delivering one here and one there and He did not wish any of His faithful people to be crushed under the wheel. Not only Jeremiah, but Baruch and a faithful remnant would be spared.

"And not faint"

The word for fainting is a strong one with a hint of cowardice or weakness in it. It means 'to fail in heart'.

124

That is where failing takes place. Prayer strengthens the heart: it comes from the heart. It is a word used by Paul:

"Therefore seeing we have this ministry, as we have received mercy, we faint not." (2 Corinthians 4:1)

"I desire that ye faint not at my tribulations."

(Ephesians 3:13)

A large part of the purpose of the parable is to help us not to faint. It is an 'end of the days' parable which means that it is applicable to our time. There must be reason therefore to believe that there is the danger of fainting in the last days. We need to take heed. Prayer is the answer for faithful men.

The Unjust Judge

This man is a double or treble picture. He is unjust; in fact, in verse 6 he is called the judge of unrighteousness (Greek). The odds against the widow were grim. This is what our world or personal circumstances are sometimes like. Life is not always fair; it does not work out that way. It almost looks as though the Lord is unfair, even though we know He is not. But life's unfairnesses are a challenge to us as they were to Daniel and Jeremiah.

In a wicked world we must expect that we shall not be treated righteously by those around us. The world is becoming more and more oppressive as we all know. The world's standards are not ours and certainly not the Lord's. More and more people do not fear God and do not fear man. They live altogether for themselves, knowingly.

The unrighteous judge in the parable is used to teach a lesson about the Judge of all the earth.

Her importunity

The widow persisted in her prayers against all odds. This was her only weapon in a world against her. The Law made it plain that God cares for widows and He had made it obligatory for Israel to do the same: "Ye shall not afflict any widow ..." (Exodus 22:22); "(God) doth execute the judgment of the fatherless and widow" (Deuteronomy 10:18). The unjust judge was altogether insensitive to anything other than his personal ends and comfort.

The widow troubled him and might weary him. "Weary" is to hit under the eye, to make one black and blue;

figuratively, to pound and pester (Paul's use is: "I keep under my body"). It was her "continual" coming that is emphasized – "men ought *always* to pray and not to faint". She had a cause and she stuck to it. Prayer was to be the answer to her abiding problem.

What was the Problem?

The cause of the woman's anxiety was an adversary from which she was desperate to be delivered: "My adversary". All of us suffer in the same way and we long to be delivered:

"Who shall deliver me from this body of death?"

(Romans 7:24, AV margin)

"Even we ourselves groan within ourselves, waiting for the adoption, to wit, the redemption of our body."

(Romans 8:23)

"Shall not God ..."

If the unrighteous judge was moved to answer by the repeated and persistent calls of a widow woman, how much more shall the righteous and merciful God answer the cries of His servants? It is unthinkable that God will do less than the unjust; surely in all His ways (as Abraham said), the Judge of all the earth shall do right. Whether it be Joseph, Naomi, Jeremiah, Israel in bondage, or the meanest servant in some obscure place, He will answer the cry.

God will not fail us. He will provide water in the thirsty land, food for the hungry, relief for His family. Every faithful prayer is heard when it is uttered and the answer is sure according to His will. God has never, never, failed any of His children. "Though it tarry, wait for it; because it will surely come, it will not tarry."

"Which cry day and night"

In crying day and night, there are echoes of Old Testament teachings: the incense morning and evening; Daniel's prayer three times a day (Daniel 6:10); David's declaration: "Evening, and morning, and at noon, will I pray, and cry aloud: and he shall hear my voice" (Psalm 55:17). We also have the repeated prayers of other faithful men:

"Lord, how long wilt thou look on? rescue my soul from their destructions, my darling from the lions ... Let not them that are mine enemies wrongfully rejoice over me." (Psalm 35:17,19)

"O God, how long shall the adversary reproach? shall the enemy blaspheme thy name for ever? Why withdrawest thou thy hand, even thy right hand? pluck it out of thy bosom." (Psalm 74:10,11)

"Lift up thyself, thou judge of the earth: render a reward to the proud. LORD, how long shall the wicked, how long shall the wicked triumph?" (Psalm 94:2,3)

"How long, O Lord, holy and true, dost thou not judge and avenge our blood on them that dwell on the earth?" (Revelation 6:10)

There is strength in prayers throughout the day – they need not always be formal. We can recall the Lord at mealtimes, as we travel, at the kitchen sink, whilst we are baking, or walking or working. It is the joy of the saints to be in instant communication with the Father through the mediation of the Lord Jesus Christ.

But the "cry" suggests deep need or deep longing. The Lord God himself has instructed us in the ceaseless petition:

"I have set watchmen upon thy walls, O Jerusalem, which shall never hold their peace day nor night: ye that make mention of the LORD (ye that are the LORD's remembrancers, RV), keep not silence, and give him no rest, till he establish, and till he make Jerusalem a praise in the earth." (Isaiah 62:6,7)

"Thy watchmen shall lift up the voice: with the voice together shall they sing: for they shall see eye to eye, when the LORD shall bring again Zion." (Isaiah 52:8)

The watchmen are obviously "his own elect" from Luke 18:7.

Paul takes up the theme of God's elect:

"Who shall lay anything to the charge of God's elect? It is God that justifieth." (Romans 8:33)

"Though he bear long with them"

What can this mean, to "bear long with them"? Is this speaking of God's patience with our shortcomings? If so, it seems to be a peculiar place to say it. Or is it bearing long with the offenders, the unrighteous, the wicked? Or is it simply saying that He has been long entreated of the elect? The word itself means 'to be long-spirited, forbearing, patient'. In the Old Testament Septuagint the word is used to mean 'longsuffering, to endure patiently'.

The RSV suggests: "Will he delay long over them?"; the NIV: "Will he keep putting them off?" The RV has: "and he is longsuffering over them."

The context is really the deciding factor because we read: "I tell you (Jesus is being personally emphatic) that he will avenge them speedily." Despite all of the seeming delay, the Lord will act promptly and well when the true moment arrives. This is much after the pattern of the experience of Daniel and Jeremiah. Habakkuk says:

"For the vision is yet for an appointed time, but at the end it shall speak (RV, it hasteth – margin, panteth – towards the end). and not lie: though it tarry, wait for it; because it will surely come, it will not tarry."
(2:3)

This verse is most apt since it refers to the Second Coming as the quotation in Hebrews 10:37 makes plain.

The difference between ourselves and the widow is that she persisted not knowing what the end would be; we persist knowing that the Lord will intervene "in the fulness of time" because God has appointed a day.

"Speedily" does not speak of rapidity in the sense of early response to prayer, but speedily when the moment arrives.

"Shall he find faith on the earth?"

This goes with the opening explanation: "Men ought always to pray, and not to faint", and suggests that many will faint. It could be taken as meaning even more than that; but the fact that it is left as a question suggests that the faith will not have died out.

As the RV margin indicates, it is: "Shall he find *the* faith? "The faith" can mean one of two things: the true faith as opposed to the false, or the faith which endures to the end.

The great widows of scripture are a living exhortation to us who are the widows of Zion, those who are waiting for the day when the Lord will put a speedy end to their widowhood in the everlasting deliverance and happiness of the kingdom on earth.

Just as the Father is God of the fatherless and widows, so our Lord is compassionate to those who recognise their need and know it can be fulfilled in him.

COMFORT OF THE SCRIPTURES

23

2nd October

1 Chronicles 16   Ezekiel 28   **Galatians 1,2**

WE have a very disconsolate but vigorous Paul who, under the Spirit, is taking the Galatians to task because they are in danger of losing the Truth. Paul says they had adopted another gospel – a hetero-gospel, as the original has it – which in fact is not another, since there cannot be any other Gospel than the good tidings from God Himself.

It was a simple but disastrous step they had taken. Some Jews, probably from Jerusalem, who were believers had persuaded them that it was essential to be circumcised and to keep the Law of Moses. This was a very persuasive argument, even though to us it might seem to be almost esoteric.

It is this that Paul tackles head-on and gives no quarter whatsoever. They are upbraided as "foolish Galatians", "bewitched", etc..

The key verse at the centre of his argument is:

"Knowing that a man is not justified by the works of the law, but by the faith of Jesus Christ, even we have believed in Jesus Christ, that we might be justified by the faith of Christ, and not by the works of the law: for by the works of the law shall no flesh be justified."

(Galatians 2:16)

This is the same as in Acts 15:

"Now therefore why tempt ye God, to put a yoke upon the neck of the disciples, which neither our fathers nor we were able to bear? But we believe that through the grace of the Lord Jesus Christ we shall be saved, even as they." (verse 10)

Today

This argument, which takes up a great deal of space in the New Testament, might seem very remote from the age in which we live. This is far from the case. It has been relevant in every age. What, circumcision and the Law? No, but the error of the principle which is: "You need Christ AND ..." to be saved.

Sometimes it is put another way round: "You need the Bible and ..." It is true in all kinds of communities: Jehovah's Witnesses, Mormons, Seventh Day Adventists, Roman Catholics, Evangelicals, Christian Scientists, etc. and it could easily happen to us.

For example, "You must have faith and the Holy Spirit in a particular form in order to be called or to understand the Bible"; or "You must have doctrine and particular beliefs about divorce and re-marriage, etc.". You can think of a dozen other things that it is easy to make into 'essentials'. These are "The Bible and ...", "Jesus and ..." philosophies. They are not for me!

But this is much more insidious than simply looking at doctrine. All of us are ever in danger of the "Jesus and ..." point of view. We load our lives with all kinds of impedimenta which we are not willing to shed – Jesus and our ambitions, Jesus and our money, Jesus and 'other' friends, Jesus and our pride, Jesus and our covetousness. When these things become 'musts' in our lives and displace Jesus only, we are right into Galatians 1 and 2.

Paul had learned the lesson in a striking way. Afterwards there was simply Jesus Christ and him crucified. "For me to live is Christ", he said.

David

Our first reading for the day is the same challenge in a different form which is worked out in David's life in a wonderful way.

You will recall that the Ark was taken captive by the Philistines in the sorry battle in the time of Samuel and Eli. It came back miraculously and rested in Kirjath Jearim for a long time. It never went back into the tabernacle which itself moved from Shiloh to Nob and then to Gibeon. The Ark was never in the tabernacle during the reigns of Saul and David.

It was David who decided that the Ark should return from Kirjath Jearim. At the first attempt, there was disaster because God killed Uzzah when he touched the falling Ark. David had created a great occasion, perhaps as a crowning piece following his double victory over the Philistines. But it was not to work out that way. They had overlooked God's requirements, and without excuse in the case of the priests and Levites who should have known better (Numbers 4).

On the second occasion there was meticulous observance of right things. From the house of Obed-Edom, the Gittite (from Gath Rimmon, a Kohathite city) the Ark came forth to sanctified priests and Levites, and words of confession and admonition from David.

But the Ark never went to the tabernacle for which it was made. It went to Jerusalem into a tent of its own in a place of its own.

The Tabernacle of David

What was the meaning of all this? How much did David understand? Certain it is that he had worked out the spiritual meanings of the things of the tabernacle and applied them to his own life – the most holy place, the laver, the altar, the incense and so on.

But when the Ark was moved to Jerusalem the second time after the death of Uzzah, David wore a linen ephod, on the lines of the priesthood though he was not a descendant of Aaron.

The tabernacle in Zion was a 'tent' (*ohel*) and not yet a dwelling place (*mishkan*).

Here was a process whereby the eventual passing of the tabernacle was anticipated: not by denouncing the Law of Moses and the ordinances of the tabernacle, but by something infinitely better – not things but a person. There is a picture of this in 1 Kings 8:4 at the inauguration of the temple built by Solomon.

***The* Tabernacle of David**

There was a man of the line of David who was also the temple of God: our Lord Jesus Christ; the one who "tabernacled amongst us" and who had himself in mind when he said, "destroy this temple ..."

This tabernacle was to 'fall down', seemingly rejected, when the Lord died at Calvary. Men thought that he was stricken of God, as though there had been another breach made as in the days of David and Uzzah.

But as Amos had foretold, the tabernacle would be rebuilt to become the permanent dwelling place of God:

"In that day will I raise up the tabernacle of David that is fallen, and close up the breaches thereof; and I will raise up his ruins, and I will build it as in the days of old." (Amos 9:11)

All of these things are anticipated in 1 Chronicles 16 and Psalm 132.

The Lord himself

Jesus was the true tabernacle of David ("I will build thee an house") in which dwelt the spiritual counterpart of the shekinah glory. The tabernacle rejected by men was made sure by the Lord God in its place, not as a tent (*ohel*) but a *mishkan*, a residence, eternally for God.

Nothing more was needed, "Neither is there salvation in any other: for there is none other name under heaven given among men, whereby we must be saved" (Acts 4:12).

But we too are the house of David, the tabernacle of David, waiting to be clothed upon with the tabernacle from heaven, the nature which is now possessed by Christ Jesus our Lord.

24

GAINING AND ATTAINING
9th October

1 Chronicles 26   Ezekiel 35   **Philippians 3,4**

PHILIPPIANS chapter 3 starts with the word "Finally" but then enters into a long digression, for which we are mightily thankful, and resumes at 4:8 with "Finally, brethren".

Paul and many of the first century believers had been greatly troubled by those who wanted Christ *and* the Law. There were influential brethren in their ranks and it was not until the Council of Jerusalem that the issue was squarely faced and resolved. Even so, the Judaisers continued to work by devious means.

While the matter is crystal clear to us, it must have been a little difficult for those who presented Moses as an obvious partner to Christ, and urged the observance of circumcision and the Law as obligatory for all – Jew and Gentile believers. You will recall that both Peter and Barnabas were wrong-footed by these powerful advocates.

Law and Grace

For Paul it was decisively clear. Between Christ and the Judaisers there was a great gulf fixed, not out of any disrespect for Moses, but because it is impossible to marry Law and Grace. The one is of works and not of faith; the other is of unmerited righteousness by faith.

Our works are our response to the grace we have received. Their works were their means of seeking to obtain eternal life by earning it. Those days are gone and we can be thankful that it is so.

Now and again, however, there are those who want to make laws for all of us to keep – not advisory ones, but compulsory laws. Many of these are well intentioned; nevertheless, the laws can be wrong in principle when they are not the things which scripture makes plain for us.

There is always a temptation to go back to law because law appears to be safe. Law defines and makes mandatory; we feel good when we keep it. The trouble about law is fourfold:

1. It produces pride.
2. It usually affects externals and does not penetrate to the heart.
3. It provides the temptation to play fast and loose with the definition.
4. No one has ever kept law perfectly except the Lord Jesus Christ. Therefore by law no one is justified.

Another and Equal Error

There are on the other hand those who mistake grace for licence. Since there are no laws, it is argued, we can do as we like and believe as we like. Everything is open. Let's discuss everything and see where we get. Let's enjoy the challenge of freedom to choose. This error is as destructive, often more so, than the first.

There is a basic flaw in all of this. There is a law which is indisputable: it is the word of God. "O how love I thy law! it is my meditation all the day." We submit to this word without question. Human reasoning is the fatal alternative to divine thought.

At the present time in our community there are those who like to think 'widely', 'liberally' and let their human minds arrive at new conclusions. The result is destructive of the faith of others and of fellowship within our brotherhood. What we need is quiet submission to the word of God – all of it – and total trust that what it teaches is right and designed to bring us to the kingdom.

Balance

The word of God is designed to keep us upright. It will keep us from veering to one side or the other in the schools of thought which appear from time to time.

Our brethren throughout the history of our community have managed to avoid the extremes by humble reading of the word of God and by prayer. Brother Robert Roberts in his exhortations in *Seasons* (and *Further Seasons*) *of Comfort* illustrates well how to keep the right ground.

Perhaps of all brethren he and Brother Islip Collyer rendered this service to all of us.

Grace exceeds Law

To return to our main theme: Paul gets to the root of the matter time and time again in all of his epistles. The difference between law and grace is the difference between flesh and spirit:

> "We are the circumcision which worship God in (by) the spirit, and rejoice in Christ Jesus, and have no confidence in the flesh." (Philippians 3:3)

"By the spirit" (as other versions make plain) does not mean that we have or need to have the Holy Spirit in order to worship. Rather, it means that our worship derives from the Spirit and not from the flesh; it is given to us by the Spirit of God in His word, and is not conceived in the mind of man.

Paul had every reason for confidence in the flesh. He was amongst the choicest of the people of God (verses 5,6). He had what many Jews envied, a pedigree and background which were impeccable. Paul could – and did in the past – preen himself on this account and in his precise observance of law. So convinced was he of his rightness, that he had been a persecutor of the ecclesia of God.

And he had been wrong. His spiritual reasoning had been distorted by his prejudices. Christ could not be Messiah otherwise the whole of his own edifice would topple. The living and risen Christ who met him on the Damascus road put an end to that. For three days Saul of Tarsus lay amongst the ruin of his earlier thinking, locked in prayer to God and convinced only that Jesus of Nazareth was God's anointed and His Son.

The Great Reappraisal

Nothing else mattered any more. Being a Hebrew, a Jew, an Israelite as the basis of salvation was up-ended. The basis was Christ: other foundation can no man lay. The rest was a write-off. The word "count", however, is not a monetary or calculating term. It means a ruling principle, the governing thought by which everything else was ruled out. If Christ is the only foundation then everything else is false.

Notice the terms "gain to me" and "loss for Christ" (verse 7). The whole perspective has changed: "me" has gone and "Christ" is there. This was true repentance and true conversion. Everything else was consigned to the rubbish heap so he might win Christ and the righteousness of God.

Is that what has happened to us? Is our thinking as clear as his? Examine yourself before this table, Christ's own table, and ask whether you have got your thinking right. Ask whether in daily life "gain(s) to me" is the over-riding guideline? It is easy in one's outlook to make "me" prominent – gains to *me*: the one who must win an argument is *me*; the one who must be the go-getter at all costs is *me*; I must emphasise my own importance and standing; I must hedge myself about with "gains" to feel secure.

Ask whether at baptism you had the right understanding in this respect. It is unlikely because it comes by deeper thought. Not all of us have the shock treatment of the Damascus Road – at least not at that point in our lives. Perhaps it comes later on. If the impact has not hit you until now, let the effect remain. Start the process. Ask if you are doing this for "gains for me" and not because you wish to "win (gain) Christ". It is an easy question and its application in daily life works wonders. It is the only way to true peace of mind. That's what Paul discovered.

It is easy to see how a wrong conclusion could be drawn. If it is by grace and not by law, by faith and not by works, by Christ and not by me – then it is all over, it is done in him.

Is salvation instant?

Paul gives the lie to that fallacy. It is he who repeatedly says we are "being saved", even in places where the AV might suggest otherwise (check against another translation, for example in 1 Corinthians 1:18). Faith is the beginning of the road; it is he who endures to the end that shall be saved. See how Paul expresses it in Philippians 3:

"If by any means I might attain unto the resurrection of the dead." (verse 11)

What does that mean? Paul was certain of resurrection from the dead because he says, "We shall all stand before the judgment seat of Christ" (Romans 14:10). What then did he mean by "if by any means I might attain"? The answer lies in verse 10. It might have puzzled you why the resurrection of Christ is mentioned before his sufferings when the sufferings came first. That is true. But it happened to Paul the other way round. It was the resurrection that convinced; it was the sufferings he had to live out in his life. So it is with us. Baptism brings about the new life because Christ is risen from the dead, but the life that follows is the "being made conformable unto his death" by the "fellowship of his sufferings".

Paul wrote:

"Ye know the grace of the Lord Jesus Christ, that, though he was rich, yet for your sakes he became poor, that ye through his poverty might be rich."
(2 Corinthians 8:9)

So we, in seeking to follow him, must ever seek the Father's will above our own, and write off our gains for "me".

An interesting word is used in Philippians 3:11 which occurs nowhere else in the New Testament. The word for resurrection here is *exanastasis,* rather than the usual *anastasis.* The prefix *ex* seems to suggest 'out of the resurrection', that is, one chosen from out of those who are raised. Comparison with the words of Jesus may lead to the same conclusion:

"But they which shall be accounted worthy to obtain that world, and the resurrection from the dead, neither marry, nor are given in marriage: neither can they die any more: for they are equal unto the angels; and are the children of God, being the children of the resurrection." (Luke 20:35,36)

"Blessed and holy is he that hath part in the first resurrection: on such the second death hath no power, but they shall be priests of God and of Christ, and shall reign with him a thousand years." (Revelation 20:6)

Pressing Upward

In keeping with "winning Christ", Paul now defines life as "one thing" (Philippians 3:13). It is like Mary's "good part" and the Psalmist's "one thing":

> "One thing have I desired of the LORD, that will I seek after; that I may dwell in the house of the LORD all the days of my life, to behold the beauty of the LORD, and to enquire in his temple."　　　　　(Psalm 27:4)

This singleness of vision ("if thine eye be single") simplifies life more than anything else. It is this which makes Paul outstanding in his service. Nothing was allowed to block his view of the mark of the prize of the upward calling in Christ Jesus. The secret lay in his mind – the mind of Christ.

Development on the Way

What is meant by: "If in any thing ye be otherwise minded, God shall reveal even this unto you" (Philippians 3:15)? Clearly Paul is saying that the true disciple develops. But is it by direct influence of the Spirit from heaven – an actual direct revelation? We all know the problems of those who claim to have direct revelations – they are usually contradictory of clear scripture. Surely, the lesson is simpler than that as in the words of Jesus: "I thank thee, O Father, Lord of heaven and earth, that thou hast hid these things from the wise and prudent, and hast revealed them unto babes" (Luke 10:21). In other words, humbling ourselves to receive the word of God will, with life's experiences, under God's hand teach us His way.

The End

Ultimately he will "change our vile body, that it may be fashioned like unto his glorious body". This is the grand consummation when all is completed. The "one thing" will then have been received: "We shall be like him."

25

SERVANTS OF THE LIVING GOD
28th October

2 Chronicles 25   **Daniel 6**   Acts 5,6

THE book of Daniel is a Spirit-provided blend of prophecy and actual life, and the two strands say the same things, but in different ways. In the one we have clear statements that God rules in the kingdoms of men, and in the other we see God actually at work on behalf of His people.

This blend is the key to our understanding and use of prophecy. There is little point in understanding all prophecy if our lives remain untouched and separate from the message that prophecy conveys. This has always been true and is becoming increasingly so as we move to the grand climax, the time when the controversy of Zion will be settled once and for all, when "the kingdoms of this world are become the kingdoms of our Lord, and of his Christ" (Revelation 11:15), when "the greatness of the kingdom under the whole heaven, shall be given to the people of the saints of the most High" (Daniel 7:27).

We are on the threshold of the time when the fabric of this civilisation will be rent to reveal the Hand behind all things and the coming of the Son of Man.

It was to Daniel that these things were vouchsafed whilst he was in the land of captivity, estranged from the land of promise and far from the holy city. He had to live by faith; he had to believe that Nebuchadnezzar, Belshazzar, Darius and Cyrus, all of whom Daniel knew personally, were in God's hand, performing His will in the furtherance of His purpose.

Daniel in a Place of Honour

In today's reading we have revealed to us once more how important and influential was Daniel's place in the life of the kingdom of Persia. Over the 127 princes or satraps were three presidents, and of the three, Daniel was preferred, distinguished; indeed, Darius was contemplating making Daniel his viceregent or viceroy.

Amongst the other presidents and princes, Daniel was envied. This was not because he was a go-getter, an aspirant for power, an ambitious, worldly man; but because his goodness and solid worth excited the jealousy of his peers. This is not an uncommon thing: Joseph was envied of his brethren, Nehemiah of his enemies, and Christ of the rulers of the Jews.

Goodness can become a cause of enmity

Daniel was a stranger, a sojourner in the land of his captivity, although by this time he was an old man and had lived in the land for seventy years. He had not become Persianised and he lived his life apart. Earlier it had been said of him:

> "There is a man in thy kingdom, in whom is the spirit of the holy gods; and in the days of thy father light and understanding and wisdom ... was found in him."
>
> (Daniel 5:11)

There was no way in which his enemies could overthrow him except by a pretext ("occasion", 6:4). By flattering the king himself and without mention of Daniel, the enemies succeeded in making it illegal for thirty days to seek petitions of anyone, gods or men, except the king.

We read in verse 7 that "all the presidents" were involved in this ploy, but it must be evident that Daniel was not included despite the eminence of his position.

Of the law of the Medes and Persians it is said that it "altereth not" (verse 8). It was an unchangeable law and could not be revoked or ignored. The king had been trapped by his servants and Daniel was ignorant of the princes' devices until the trap was sprung. Meanwhile they had been forced to say amongst themselves:

> "We shall not find any occasion against this Daniel, except we find it against him concerning the law of his God."
>
> (6:5)

In other words, they had unwittingly decided to fight against God! The writing of the king had been set against the writing of the word of God. Time and again men have set themselves against the word of God – Pharaoh, Nabal,

Ahab, Caiaphas and many others – only to destroy themselves. The wisdom of men is foolishness to God and "he taketh the wise in their own craftiness".

Daniel is called "this Daniel' (verse 5) and "that Daniel, which is of the children of the captivity" (verse 13). This is in great contrast to God's own assessment of the man: "Thou art greatly beloved" (9:23; 10:11,19). "Greatly beloved" has particular significance. The word comes from a root meaning 'to delight in'. It is translated variously, including: beauty, delectable thing, (great) delight, pleasant, precious. What men might think of us is of no account; what the Lord God thinks is everything.

The Vital Decision

Daniel was accustomed to praying three times a day. Nothing in the business of the king was more important than the business of the King of Heaven. The stranger in a strange land had his mind on the Land of Promise and on the Holy City of God. He had studied the Law and the Prophets and knew what the Lord would do and when. The Lord's decree, unlike that of the Medes and Persians, could not be set aside because none is greater or more faithful than He.

Daniel's habit of prayer was known to others. His faith was manifest and constant; it was known amongst the princes and to the king Darius. Daniel was a great man of prayer and his prayers were centred on the promises of God. It was not for himself that he prayed – he was never to return to the Land, but, like Moses, he would die outside it.

His windows had always been open towards Jerusalem at his hours of prayer:

"If I forget thee, O Jerusalem, let my right hand forget her cunning. If I do not remember thee, let my tongue cleave to the roof of my mouth; if I prefer not Jerusalem above my chief joy."   (Psalm 137:5,6)

"I have set watchmen upon thy walls, O Jerusalem, which shall never hold their peace day nor night: ye that make mention of the LORD, keep not silence, and give him no rest, till he establish, and till he make Jerusalem a praise in the earth."   (Isaiah 62:6,7)

The Eyes of the LORD are in every place

With vipers' tongues the plotters revealed that Daniel had broken the law of the Medes and Persians. They believed that Daniel was now irrevocably taken in the web they had so carefully spun:

"They hatch cocatrice' eggs, and weave the spider's web: he that eateth of their eggs dieth, and that which is crushed breaketh out into a viper. Their webs shall not become garments, neither shall they cover themselves with their works: their works are works of iniquity, and the act of violence is in their hands. Their feet run to evil, and they make haste to shed innocent blood."   (Isaiah 59:5-7)

"He lieth in wait secretly as a lion in his den: he lieth in wait to catch the poor: he doth catch the poor, when he draweth him into his net."   (Psalm 10:9)

"For without cause have they hid for me their net in a pit, which without cause they have digged for my soul. Let destruction come upon him at unawares; and let his net that he hath hid catch himself; into that very destruction let him fall. And my soul shall be joyful in the LORD: it shall rejoice in his salvation. All my bones shall say, LORD, who is like unto thee, which deliverest the poor from him that is too strong for him, yea, the poor and the needy from him that spoileth him?"
(Psalm 35:7-10)

The king was distressed beyond measure, and like Pilate, though sincerely, he knew that there was no fault at all in this man. Nevertheless, to the delight of the onlooking satraps and princes, Daniel the aged and the righteous, was brought forth and cast into the den of lions, but not before the king in a remarkable display of confidence and in a personal witness to the character of his servant had said:

"Thy God whom thou servest continually, he will deliver thee."   (Daniel 6:16)

The word, "continually" means enduringly, permanently and comes from a root which means 'to dwell'.

"He that dwelleth in the secret place of the most High shall abide under the shadow of the Almighty. I will say

144

of the LORD, He is my refuge and my fortress: my God; in him will I trust. Surely he shall deliver thee from the snare of the fowler." (Psalm 91:1-3)

It would seem that the princes did not trust the king or the lions! They sealed the den with a stone and with the king's and their own signets. The king passed a restless night and denied himself the usual sensual pleasures. What the princes thought, we do not know. There would have been a feeling of unease. Past history of the fiery furnace would not be unknown to them, and, moreover, they had seen the deportment of the man they had betrayed. Perhaps there are parallels with events described in our New Testament readings for today:

"All that sat in the council, looking stedfastly on him, saw his face as it had been the face of an angel." (Acts 6:15)

There is no recorded word of Daniel; no plea, no complaint. He also was "brought as a lamb to the slaughter, and as a sheep before her shearers is dumb, so he openeth not his mouth" (Isaiah 53:7).

Morning Light

The sun was rising over the city and plain when the king hastened to the den of lions. Despite all that he had said to Daniel the day before, he was filled with doubt, and in a lamentable ('afflicted, worried, pained') voice, he cried:

"O Daniel, servant of the living God, is thy God, whom thou servest continually, able to deliver thee from the lions?" (Daniel 6:20)

The sad cry of the king revealed a great deal concerning the character of Daniel and of the king's knowledge of Daniel's God ("the living God"). "Is thy God able?" was a question that was unnecessary concerning the One who can say, "Is anything too hard for me?" And for us in our day the assurance is tremendous:

"(Neither) height, nor depth, nor any other creature, shall be able to separate us from the love of God, which is in Christ Jesus our Lord." (Romans 8:39)

"Now unto him that is able to do exceeding abundantly above all that we ask or think ..." (Ephesians 3:20)

"For I know whom I have believed, and am persuaded that he is able to keep that which I have committed unto him against that day." (2 Timothy 1:12)

"For in that he himself hath suffered being tempted, he is able to succour them that are tempted."
(Hebrews 2:18)

"Wherefore he is able also to save them to the uttermost that come unto God by him, seeing he ever liveth to make intercession for them." (Hebrews 7:25)

"Now unto him that is able to keep you from falling, and to present you faultless before the presence of his glory with exceeding joy ..." (Jude verse 24)

Daniel's Words

To the king's relief, Daniel replied:

"My God hath sent his angel, and hath shut the lions' mouths ... forasmuch as before him innocency was found in me." (Daniel 6:22)

The divine commentary is that:

"No manner of hurt was found upon him, because he believed in his God." (verse 23)

These words go with:

"who through faith ... stopped the mouths of lions."
(Hebrews 11:33)

The Other Daniel

Everything in the record is a prefiguring of the work and experience of the Lord Jesus Christ. In Daniel there is no error, no fault, no recorded sin. His only 'crime' was in obeying the law of his God. But in Persia there was a law of sin and death from which there was no escape. Yet Daniel did escape because he was beloved of God. The terrors of the tomb, the stone across the mouth of the lions' den, the seal, were all overcome, as they were in the later fulfilment in Golgotha. Very early in the morning the king found Daniel saved from typical death. Early in the morning they found the tomb of the Son of the living God, empty. Stones and seals were useless against the power of God. Why will they never learn?

146

Finally

We too are the servants of the living God; we are the ecclesia of the living God. We have been sealed with the seal of the living God (Revelation 7:3). We too have been delivered 'out of the mouth of the lion' that will devour the adversaries; and we are rejoicing in the Lion of the tribe of Judah.

COMFORT OF THE SCRPTURES

26

"I COMMEND YOU TO GOD"
7th November

2 Chronicles 36 **Hosea 4** **Acts 20**

THERE are times in our daily readings when as we finish the chapters we sigh over the infinite mercy of God and the unregenerate wickedness of some of His people. It seems unbelievable that man could be so perverse, and all to his own destruction. As we reach the end of the Chronicles of the Kingdom of God in the Old Testament, the comment on His people's behaviour is inevitable:

"And the LORD God of their fathers sent to them by his messengers, rising up betimes, and sending; because he had compassion on his people, and on his dwelling place: but they mocked the messengers of God, and despised his words, and misused his prophets, until the wrath of the LORD arose against his people, till there was no remedy [margin, healing]."

(2 Chronicles 36:15,16)

Through the prophets who were so misused and despised, God also revealed the fundamental problem:

"Hear the word of the LORD, ye children of Israel: for the LORD hath a controversy with the inhabitants of the land, because there is no truth, nor mercy, nor knowledge of God in the land." (Hosea 4:1)

Knowledge of God and His word were seriously deficient in these people who marked the end of their generation, in both Judah and Israel.

We are nearing the end of a generation and have to heed the advice given to the early disciples to "save yourselves from this untoward generation". There is something about human nature which, despite frequent and clear warning, presses on in its foolishness, hasting towards an inevitable destruction.

149

Take heed

The situation was no different in the first century, when the Apostle called the Ephesian elders to meet him at Miletus. His message was grave and serious:

"Therefore watch, and remember, that by the space of three years I ceased not to warn every one night and day with tears." (Acts 20:31)

Paul, like his Master, warned the believers of his day about the dangers that lay ahead for them. They could never say they had not been warned.

So it is with us. The last days are vividly described and we know that our generation fits the description. Let us note part of the warning: Watch and remember, said Paul.

The word 'watch' comes from a word which speaks of being aroused from sleep, a theme common in Paul's writings:

"Therefore let us not sleep, as do others; but let us watch and be sober. For they that sleep sleep in the night; and they that be drunken are drunken in the night. But let us, who are of the day, be sober, putting on the breastplate of faith and love; and for an helmet, the hope of salvation. For God hath not appointed us to wrath, but to obtain salvation by our Lord Jesus Christ." (1 Thessalonians 5:6-9)

"And that, knowing the time, that now it is high time to awake out of sleep: for now is our salvation nearer than when we believed. The night is far spent, the day is at hand: let us therefore cast off the works of darkness, and let us put on the armour of light." (Romans 13:11,12)

We cannot say we have not been warned, nor can we claim that we do not know that one of the high risk factors is that we shall fall asleep – be unconscious of what is going on. It was exactly that situation that befell the apostles in Gethsemane, though doubtless they had more reason for the failure than we could adduce:

"Watch ye and pray, lest ye enter into temptation. The spirit truly is ready, but the flesh is weak." (Mark 14:38)

There are three points to note: one we can do nothing about; the other two lie within our powers: the weakness of our flesh, watchfulness and prayer.

"Therefore let us not sleep, as do others; but let us watch and be sober." (1 Thessalonians 5:6) Again there are three points: beware of sleep – which is the counterpart of the weakness of the flesh; watch individually and collectively; and sobriety, meaning to be temperate, circumspect, calm, collected.

"But the end of all things is at hand: be ye therefore sober, and watch unto prayer." (1 Peter 4:7) Peter uses another word for 'sober', meaning to be in the right mind, sound, exercising self-control.

"Watch ye, stand fast in the faith, quit you like men, be strong." (1 Corinthians 16:13)

"Continue in prayer, and watch in the same with thanksgiving." (Colossians 4:2) Here are three more points to note: this time, all are spiritual antidotes to slumber: continuance in prayer, watchfulness in prayer, and thanksgiving.

"Remember therefore how thou hast received and heard, and hold fast, and repent. If therefore thou shalt not watch, I will come on thee as a thief, and thou shalt not know what hour I will come upon thee." (Revelation 3:3) Watching and remembrance are once more linked together. We cannot remember what we do not know. We ought to know. It is what we have received and heard – that is what we remember.

Remember

The word for 'remember' is the verb for the device we sometimes use to remember things – *mnemonic*. It means to be mindful, to make mention.

"And truly, if they had been mindful of that country from whence they came out, they might have had opportunity to have returned." (Hebrews 11:15) "Been mindful" is another verb from the same noun. All of us are remembering many different things all day long. We always remember what is important to us. If,

151

therefore, we forget the food of life it is because it has not occupied the prime place that it should have in our minds.

I commend you

Paul told the elders of Ephesus that they would not be left to their own devices in the fight against slumber. There is spiritual food to give spiritual strength:

"And now, brethren, I commend you to God, and to the word of his grace, which is able to build you up, and to give you an inheritance among all them which are sanctified." (Acts 20:32)

"Commend" means 'to commit to the keeping of'.

"Wherefore let them that suffer according to the will of God commit the keeping of their souls to him in well-doing, as unto a faithful Creator." (1 Peter 4:19)

He is able ...

Paul's message was that the strength Christ's followers need is available from God. Think of the times that Christ's ability to help is mentioned:

"Now unto him *that is able* to keep you from falling, and to present you faultless before the presence of his glory with exceeding joy." (Jude verse 24)

"For the which cause I also suffer these things: nevertheless I am not ashamed: for I know whom I have believed, and am persuaded that *he is able* to keep that which I have committed unto him against that day." (2 Timothy 1:12)

"For in that he himself hath suffered being tempted, *he is able* to succour them that are tempted." (Hebrews 2:18)

"Wherefore *he is able* also to save them to the uttermost that come unto God by him, seeing he ever liveth to make intercession for them." (Hebrews 7:25)

"Who shall change our vile body, that it may be fashioned like unto his glorious body, according to the working whereby *he is able* even to subdue all things unto himself." (Philippians 3:21)

The reading from Acts also spoke of God's word being "able":

"And now, brethren, I commend you to God, and to the word of his grace, which is able to build you up, and to give you an inheritance among all them which are sanctified." (Acts 20:32)

We can receive the same help promised by Paul to those in first century Ephesus. God's word remains the source of information about His purpose, and through its message we can come to know Him and His Son. Failure to appreciate the Father and His ways led to the captivity and destruction of God's people, whose history has been recorded for our admonition, on whom the end of the present age has come. God's word can build us up.

"Build you up" means to build upon an established foundation, which is faith in Christ Jesus:

"Built upon the foundation of the apostles and prophets, Jesus Christ himself being the chief corner stone." (Ephesians 2:20)

"Rooted and built up in him, and stablished in the faith, as ye have been taught, abounding therein with thanksgiving." (Colossians 2:7)

"But ye, beloved, building up yourselves on your most holy faith, praying in the Holy Spirit." (Jude verse 20)

The inheritance as heirs

Paul then showed the reward that is planned for all who are faithful: the hope of being joint-heirs with Christ.

"The eyes of your understanding being enlightened; that ye may know what is the hope of his calling, and what the riches of the glory of his inheritance in the saints." (Ephesians 1:18)

"Knowing that of the Lord ye shall receive the reward of the inheritance: for ye serve the Lord Christ." (Colossians 3:24)

"And for this cause he is the mediator of the new testament, that by means of death, for the redemption of the transgressions that were under the first testament, they which are called might receive the promise of eternal inheritance." (Hebrews 9:15)

The promise was part of the exceeding great and precious promises given to Abraham:

153

"By faith Abraham, when he was called to go out into a place which he should after receive for an inheritance, obeyed; and he went out, not knowing whither he went."

(Hebrews 11:8)

Strengthen according to thy word

As we come round the Lord's table, we reflect again on all that he did. We are, as it were, with the disciples in Gethsemane, witnessing his struggle against the final, great temptation: "The spirit is willing but the flesh is weak". Too often, like them, we fail to be alert, watching and praying. Thankfully, we are not left alone:

"Wait on the LORD: be of good courage, and he shall strengthen thine heart: wait, I say, on the LORD."

(Psalm 27:14)

"My soul melteth for heaviness: strengthen thou me according unto thy word." (Psalms 119:28)

God did not leave His Son alone; He heard the prayer, and responded immediately:

The Father heard; an angel there
Sustained the Son of God in prayer,
   In sad Gethsemane;
He drank the dreadful cup of pain,
Then rose to life and joy again.

27

HELPS

22nd November

Nehemiah 10   **Amos 2**   **1 Timothy 4,5**

WHEN doing our readings day by day, it sometimes seems that we are very small and insignificant people compared with those we are reading about – Nehemiah, Amos, and Paul and Timothy, for example. And this is true: it requires some big people for the extra special tasks that are laid upon them. But big people require little people to help them, and, in fact, they could not do without them.

We all need each other. It is right that we should think of ourselves as we truly are – little people. But we must not be discouraged, nor under-estimate our work as though everything would go on just the same without us.

The Altar Fire

The brazen altar in the tabernacle was an essential part of the furniture of worship and without it the work of the tabernacle could not take place. It was in use every day, right from the first lamb that was offered first thing in the morning, to the last lamb that was offered at the end of the day.

But the offerings of the lambs would have been useless without the fire by which they were consumed and the smoke that ascended up to heaven. The words 'burnt offering' are literally, 'the ascending' – almost like a stairway to heaven.

The fire had been kindled in the first place direct from heaven:

"And there came a fire out from before the LORD, and consumed upon the altar the burnt offering and the fat: which when all the people saw, they shouted, and fell on their faces."   (Leviticus 9:24)

And it was commanded that the fire was not to be allowed to go out:

"The fire shall ever be burning upon the altar; it shall never go out." (Leviticus 6:13)

But to keep the fire alight, it was necessary that there should be a constant supply of wood available for the priests to use. Who collected the wood?

The Little People

Special provision was made for the collection of wood. This is mentioned in today's reading from Nehemiah:

"And we cast the lots among the priests, the Levites, and the people, for the wood offering, to bring it into the house of our God, after the houses of our fathers, at times appointed year by year, to burn upon the altar of the LORD our God, as it is written in the law." (Nehemiah 10:34)

Everyone was to provide some wood and this was done by a roster system among the priests, Levites and people. They brought the wood at times appointed, year by year. From all over the country, wood would come to the temple to keep the altar fire burning. From the land of rich and poor, near and far, supplies would reach the temple at appointed times.

Thus it was that those who, because they were not priests or Levites, were not able to work in the temple could nevertheless support a major task without which the temple could not function.

The Wood Offering

Furthermore, the wood was called "the wood offering". The word 'offering' is the ordinary word for offerings – burnt offerings, peace offerings, etc. In other words, it was accepted by God as an offering at the altar. This is a remarkable fact. However ordinary and undistinguished the one who brought the wood, his wood was accepted as an offering to God as surely as the other offerings were accepted – indeed, his work was an essential part of the whole. Everything that touched the altar was made holy, and this must have applied to the wood as well.

It will have been noted that the wood was brought according to lot at the appointed times, not simply when the offerer felt like it. Everything had to be done decently and in order.

Furthermore when the wood was used, it had to be laid "in order":

"And the sons of Aaron the priest shall put fire upon the altar, and lay the wood in order upon the fire." (Leviticus 1:7)

This same care was shown by Abraham who laid the wood "in order" when offering Isaac, and by Elijah who also laid the wood "in order" in the great offering on Mount Carmel. Even the ashes that were left were taken outside the camp to a clean place.

Ourselves

Thus our own small portions in ecclesial service, however small they are, are essential parts of the whole. They are rendered holy because we offer them in the name of Christ our altar.

And, when we die, we are placed as it were in a clean place, a place associated with the altar even though it is in some distant spot on earth. It is known of God.

We must never under-estimate the worth of our part and we must never render it in a slovenly, ill-prepared way. Everything must be done decently and in order.

Helps

In the first century, for the maintenance of the ecclesia in the days before there was a complete Bible, God gave spirit gifts by the Holy Spirit to individual members of the ecclesia. One of these gifts was quite astonishing in its simplicity:

"And God hath set some in the church, first apostles, secondarily prophets, thirdly teachers, after that miracles, then gifts of healings, *helps*, governments, diversities of tongues." (1 Corinthians 12:28)

There it is – "helps". Whoever had this gift was able to render special help to others whatever their work. What a marvellous thing to be able to help others!

What is more, God considered this to be an essential part of the work. in every ecclesia large or small there are those who are "helps". These are the ones who oil the wheels to make them go round.

I was at a meeting where a blind brother was speaking. He knew what he was talking about but he needed help when it came to reading from the scriptures, and he had another brother with him whose job it was to turn up the passage and read it. Here was the help. Helps are a form of partnership, like those who turn over the pages of music for the pianist. They seem to be small jobs, but they are nevertheless essential, and therefore, have an importance of their own.

Paul says:

> "Salute Urbane, our helper in Christ, and Stachys my beloved." (Romans 16:9)

God needs help

God needs help? In a sense, yes. Of course, it is not that God cannot achieve His purpose because He is too weak, but it does mean that there are things given to us to do which are essential to His purpose:

> "Curse ye Meroz, said the angel of the LORD, curse ye bitterly the inhabitants thereof; because they came not to the help of the LORD, to the help of the LORD against the mighty." (Judges 5:23)

God gives help

Thankfully, God gives help:

> "So that we may boldly say, The Lord is my helper, and I will not fear what man shall do unto me." (Hebrews 13:6)

28

ESTHER: WOMAN OF FAITH
29th November
Esther 5,6   Amos 9   Hebrews 1,2

THE kingdom of Medo-Persia was at its height. The record says there were 127 provinces, 120 of which are mentioned in Daniel 6:1, plus seven princes in Esther 1:14. The Jews were those or the children of those who had not elected to go back to the Land. They were now resident in Persia as another 'home'.

It was a massive kingdom stretching to the borders of India in the east and to Europe in the west. The Jews were strangers and scattered abroad. They had no temple or central meeting place, but it would appear that synagogues became a part of life – not that they are mentioned in the book of Esther.

If synagogues were not the means of keeping their faith alive, it must have been the strength of the family bond. Probably, both. The family would preserve the knowledge that they were exiles from the Land and were the children of Abraham and of God. Presumably the boys were circumcised and there must have been a copy of the Law somewhere amongst them.

Absorption? Assimilation?

There is always the risk when we are separated from our brethren and sisters in some way that we find friends and pleasures in the world around us. That would be easy in one sense in Singapore* because the government has sought to preserve the sense of family, being Singaporeans, in a whole variety of ways. The Lord Jesus has told us that we are in the world but we are not to be of it. We cannot help being in the world in the sense of living in it; but we can help being a part of the world in its habits and pursuits.

---

* Exhortation given in Singapore, 29th November, 1998.

That was the challenge in Britain during the war. Government had to keep the nation informed and encouraged to keep up morale, despite what was going on in the battlefields.

There were things by which we were kept separate. We were conscientious objectors and had to stand for our faith before tribunals and against the mocking or disdain by some of the people.

The Jews

The Jews were kept on their toes by the fact that anti-Semitism was never very far away. It continues to be like that in so many places.

In Persia there were many Jews who, for one reason or another, had not returned to the Land following Cyrus' decree saying that they were free to return. Daniel remained behind because God had placed him there. Others, perhaps, were by this time so well at home in Persia that the return to Israel would – apart from spiritual reasons – have seemed to be disadvantageous so far as human comfort was concerned.

In the time of Jesus many Jews lived outside the Land in the Diaspora and were able, because of their merchanting skills, to make a comfortable living, and had the local synagogue which helped them keep together in the Jewish faith and nationality.

The tide turns

We can never be sure when the tide will turn. We tend to think that everything will continue as it is, although we have been warned by God not to rely on the world or its people for support in spiritual things.

The tide turned in Persia. The monarch had complete control; he was very rich and loved in various ways to display his possessions and wealth. The prolonged feast in Esther 1 is such an example.

For whatever reason, the queen Vashti refused the command of the king to parade herself and display her beauty. She was with her ladies and did not want to be demeaned before guests at the feast at the command of the king. Perhaps there was more to it than that.The king and his seven wise men used this as an occasion to assert the rights of men (without regard to their wives). It cost Vashti her crown.

God works

But this occasion was to draw God's people to Him and Esther was both the example and means to accomplish this task.

The virgins throughout the empire came under scrutiny and those who were pleasing to the eye, irrespective of class and, perhaps, character, were taken to Susa where the eunuchs appointed to the task groomed and developed the virgins under their care.

Esther was the cousin, perhaps niece, of Mordecai. She was brought up by him and was obedient as though she were his daughter. Her name means 'star', or by extension Venus; his name means 'a little man' or, perhaps, 'dedicated to Mars'. He appears to have had a post in the outer court of the palace at Susa.

Providentially, all of this was because of God's purpose. We need to remember that the angels are at work today and always, and may not know beforehand what they are accomplishing for God.

Separation

The king's desire for a queen led to Esther, a beautiful young woman, being selected for the harem. The king did not know that he was a tool in God's hand. Esther found favour and did not reveal her nationality at any time prior to her selection as queen. If we ask why, we are told that it was at the command of Mordecai. What purpose did he have in mind – simply to have Esther as queen? He was a godly man and must have been seeking to do the will of God.

Just when Haman came into his purview, we are not told. This man was an Amalekite, probably a descendant of Agag of Samuel's time – part of the perpetual enemy of the Lord God.

Mordecai, a godly man, did not show reverence for Haman as he, increasing in favour with the king, looked for everyone to bow down to him. There must have been something which made it impossible for Mordecai's conscience to do this even though he was risking his life.

Haman could have dealt with Mordecai at any time but his vanity would not allow him to stoop to deal with one offender. Mordecai had not hidden the fact that he was a Jew. That was enough to cause Haman's wicked mind to get to work. He already knew that the Jews were everywhere in the kingdom and had their own religious laws. The Jews were different and Mordecai was an archetypal victim of anti-Semitism.

Despite his observations and detective work, Haman had not thought it necessary to seek to learn who Esther the queen really was. Nor had the messengers who sought her out in the beginning. They do not seem to have noted the kind of home they were taking her from.

Like Hitler in the Second World War, Haman's plan was also his death warrant. The word was still true: "He that curseth thee I will curse". God's word never fails.

Like all chastisement for discerning men, his wicked plan was also the means of drawing the Jews closer together and doubtless to their God, though He is not named specifically in the book. It could be that the reason for this suppression of His name from the book was to tell us that God is at work nevertheless. In our own day we too live in a time when there are no prophets and no open vision, but it is clear that He is at work.

Timing

The plot was hatched and decided in the month Nisan which is the month Abib, the month of the Passover. For every Jew this date would be burned into their hearts. It was the time when the nation truly came into being.

The edict was published and like all the laws of the Medes and Persians became irrevocable. The dreadful news was carried to the ends of the empire. In Susa it caused Mordecai to don sackcloth as he sat in the outer court, so he was noted by Haman as he passed in and out and he must have gloated over Mordecai's sorrow and was happy to bide his time until the month Adar.

News of Mordecai's behaviour reached Esther and she sent clothes for Mordecai to wear but, knowing her motives were good, Mordecai told Esther to make it known

162

that she was a Jewess by seeking audience of the king. She had not been with the king for thirty days.

Now she had a copy of the decree sent by Mordecai with the message that she was not to cherish the idea that as queen she would escape. Mordecai widened her mind to one of fellowship with and for her people. As Mordecai had risked his life by disdaining to reverence Haman, so Esther was commanded to come out into the open because, who knows whether she was queen because God had placed her there for this very purpose. Whether that be so or not, if she failed, she would not escape, and God would raise a deliverer from another quarter.

Esther had always been obedient to Mordecai and she now rose to this challenge. Mordecai and his fellow Jews were to join Esther and her maidens for a three-day fast after which Esther would go uninvited to the king. Perhaps she prayed that she might be called of him without her having to risk her life. Be that as it may, she was resolved in her mind that she would go to the outer court and "If I perish, I perish". She was willing to be faithful unto death.

As she stood in the outer court, the king lifted his eyes. He could have been anywhere in Susa or his empire but that day he was on his throne. He extended his golden sceptre to Esther and touching the top she must have praised and thanked her God.

Slowly the net was closing on Haman and he did not yet know it. He was in greater favour than ever and more was to come because he had been invited with the king to the queen's banquet! Esther bided her time. Another banquet the following night was all she asked, although the king had offered her anything up to the half of his kingdom!

Haman walked on air or rode jauntily home to tell his wife all about the honour bestowed on him. He celebrated in his exuberance, but told his wife that despite all this happiness, he found the very sight of Mordecai as gall to his stomach. Haman was persuaded, though he required little of that, to erect gallows for Mordecai, gallows seventy-five feet high! He was to ask the king next day whether he might be rid of Mordecai.

Victory by insomnia!

The angel must have been delighted to visit the king in secret and disturb his sleep! Victory by insomnia! The king asked for a book of records and there was handed to him, again doubtless by the angel's urging, that very section in which Mordecai's name was favourably mentioned because he had passed information about the treachery of two of the king's chamberlains. Mordecai's warning proved to be the king's deliverance but the king had not rewarded the faithful Jew. He would do so now!

Haman was already in the outer court early in the morning – a diligent worker – and he was summoned by the king. His ego imagined that the question the king asked him was about his own honour and therefore he lavished honour on himself in his imagination. But, alas for him, the recipient was to be none other than Mordecai and he was designated to ensure that everything in his answer to the king was to be given to Mordecai. Imagine the scene when Mordecai's sackcloth was covered by the royal apparel, the regal robe, and he was lifted on to the royal horse and taken through the city to the cry, "Bow the knee"! Bow the knee to my enemy, the one who refused to bow to me!

Haman knew in his heart, and his wife and friends reinforced his fears, that his doom was now sealed and that night after the banquet he was hurried to the seventy-five-foot gallows and strung up.

So it was that the Jews were able to countermand the edict of Haman that had been sealed with the king's seal, and fight for themselves to great effect, being doubtless strengthened by the hand of the Lord. Annually the Jews were to remember Purim as they do to this day. First Passover and then Purim. Mordecai who had been humiliated by Haman was now in royal favour.

So it can be for us. The Man who rose from his signet-sealed tomb will exalt us if in this our age we remember him week by week, and continue to be a separate people for him in hope of the Great Day when the edict of death will be overpowered by the One who has immortality for us.

29

"THE GLORY THAT SHALL BE REVEALED"
13th December

Job 15   Habakkuk 2   **1 Peter 3-5**

THE theme for this exhortation is taken from 1 Peter 5:1 in which Peter is exhorting his fellow elders whilst we are allowed to overhear him.

Peter has been a witness of great things – the sufferings and the glory of Christ. We can only surmise the occasions when he saw these things. Does it mean that, despite his denials, Peter came out to see what was happening to his Master in his time of suffering? And the glory; when was this? Was it by seeing the risen Christ? Or was it a reminder of the transfiguration?

These two aspects go hand in hand: sufferings and glory; the cross before the crown; "But the God of all grace ... after that ye have suffered a while, make you perfect" (verse 10); "We must through much tribulation enter into the kingdom of God" (Acts 14:22). All of these things are true.

Peter is saying that he was a witness and a partaker of the glory. It is true that the glory of the transfiguration enveloped them as though they were part of the scene, and intrinsically it held the promise that the faithful three, Peter, James and John, would inherit the glory with Christ in the kingdom.

Is there a sense in which we now are partakers of the glory? The answer clearly is yes. Earlier in Peter we read:

"Whom having not seen, ye love; in whom, though now ye see him not, yet believing, ye rejoice with joy unspeakable and full of glory."   (1 Peter 1:8)

The glory of Christ comprises the glory bestowed on him by the Father and it will be manifest in his bride. That glory has touched us in that we have been taught these things and we believe them with all our hearts, and at every breaking of bread we express this faith – faith in the

165

promise of the words from Christ: "I will not drink thereof until it be fulfilled in the kingdom of God".

Every breaking of bread is itself a prophecy of the day when we shall truly all be one bread, when God gathers together in one all things in Christ.

Humility

Peter says something which the AV does not fully bring out in the phrase "be subject one to another, and be clothed with humility" (1 Peter 5:5). The word "clothed" means to be girt about, as a slave with his apron. Here was Peter, by the Spirit, being reminded of the time when Christ was girded with a towel and Peter in self-assurance contradicted his Lord.

Humility is the badge of discipleship, whether we be old or young, man or wife, arranging brethren or otherwise. There is no glory to come if there is no humility now. Arrogance, self-assertion, one-up-man-ship should have no part in the character of the disciple of Christ. Remember the towel for which the word in John 13 is the same as for the apron of the slave. It is not simply that we are to be subject one to another; it is also:

"Humble yourselves therefore under the mighty hand of God, that he may exalt you in due time."   (verse 6)

No humility; no glory

The glory that Moses gained by his time in Mount Sinai faded away. That was the glory of the law. But the law that is grace is "eternal glory". God has called us to eternal glory by Christ Jesus or as Paul wrote it:

"Obtain the salvation which is in Christ Jesus with eternal glory."   (2 Timothy 2:10)

What is this glory

Surely there will be radiance and light, but of themselves these do not speak of the substance of this glory (literally, 'weight' – *kabod*). There is no glory but of God:

"We beheld his glory, the glory as of the only begotten of the Father."   (John 1:14)

We are told that Christ will return in the glory of the Father. This is the Father's response to all who faithfully seek to honour Him in life by trying to be Godlike. In the

166

kingdom we shall have the divine glory, we shall have the divine nature.

The Crown

"When the chief Shepherd shall appear, ye shall receive a crown of glory that fadeth not away."

(1 Peter 5:4)

The Pope has a triple crown, a fake, a blasphemous crown. The one for the saints is the *stephanos*, the victor's crown, equivalent to the garland received by the winner of the games. It is indeed the triple crown, the crown of glory, the crown of life and the crown of righteousness.

Thus there is a marvellous blessing for the saints of God – for you, if you really believe and seek to do His will. There is no point in breaking bread unless we truly believe that this is what the Lord God wishes us to have. It is all a part of the glory that shall be revealed; it is the joy unspeakable and full of glory. Then the saints will be glad with exceeding joy. It is not a dream or a wish; it is a promise sealed with the blood of the One who first wore a crown of thorns.

There is a wonderful passage in Revelation 4:10,11:

"The four and twenty elders fall down before him that sat on the throne, and worship him that liveth for ever and ever, and cast their crowns before the throne, saying, Thou art worthy, O Lord, to receive glory and honour and power: for thou hast created all things, and for thy pleasure they are and were created."

There is one final point of beauty to notice. It is found in Isaiah 62:3. Jerusalem, especially the heavenly Jerusalem, "shalt also be a crown of glory (beauty) in the hand of the LORD, and a royal diadem in the hand of thy God".

Why? And for whom is this crown? Surely for none other than the Lamb, the Bridegroom. He will be the crown with the Bride he has won for himself, and together in mutual glory, they will display the glory of the Father, the glory that shall be revealed, the eternal glory, in everlasting joy.

167

COMFORT OF THE SCRIPTURES

30

HOW CAN A MAN BE RIGHTEOUS?
20th December

Job 25-27   **Zechariah 3**   **Jude**

DESPITE all of the their differences, it is clear that Job and his friends have a common problem. Eliphaz asks:

"Shall mortal man be more just than God? Shall a man be more pure than his maker?"   (4:17)

Job also asks:

"How should a man be just with God?"   (9:2)

Again Eliphaz queries:

"What is man, that he should be clean? and he which is born of a woman, that he should be righteous?"   (15:14)

Bildad now poses the same question:

"How then can man be justified with God? or how can he be clean that is born of a woman?"   (25:4)

This a question which lies deeper than the burning issue of suffering which at first appears to be the question in the book of Job.

The cry for a Daysman

Job feels so sure that there is no cause attributable to his sufferings (and in one sense he is right – his problem is that he defends himself to the extent that he attributes blame to God; and there Job cannot be right). This causes Job to wish for a Daysman between himself and God. This raises a very interesting subject because in one sense it is the Bible-long question of law and grace.

Look at the verses involved:

"Neither is there any daysman betwixt us, that might lay his hand upon us both."   (9:33)

You will see that the margin renders "daysman" as "umpire", meaning a referee, an arbitrator. Job felt that

169

this held the solution to his problem and would both silence his friends and put the position right with God.

The word for "daysman" occurs in various forms in Job and it is instructive to examine some of them:

"But what doth your arguing reprove? Do ye imagine to reprove words?" (6:25,26)

Here the words, "arguing" and "reprove" are the daysman word.

"Surely I would speak with the Almighty, and I desire to reason with God." (13:3)

Here it is the word "reason" that is also translated "daysman".

"But I will *maintain* mine own ways before him." (13:15)

"Should he *reason* with unprofitable talk?" (15:3)

"O that one might *plead* for a man with God."(16:21)

In these passages, the words "maintain", "reason" and "plead", are all this word "daysman."

From all of these it is clear that the meaning lies in seeking to be right by proof of argument because one is sure of one's case. What Job learns at the end, and what we all know because Scripture has made it abundantly plain, is that there is no future for us down that road. If God were to demand it we would always lose our case. There is no one so righteous as He – always. We don't want a daysman. Conscience tells us that a daysman would find us in the wrong, and God in the right.

Job's friends were wrong because they singled Job out from the rest of them and made him the butt of their "daysman" arguing without realising that "all are guilty before God".

The Redeemer

But Job came to another solution which, however dimly he perceived it or however clearly, is the real answer to the need of man. This is the everlasting comfort, the whole remedy; and what is more it is provided by the One who could have insisted on the Daysman, the arguer, the reprover – and who would have won every time.

The book of Job appears to be one of the oldest books of the Bible. It is likely that Job lived around the time of Abraham. His age span, the mention of Uz which occurs in the book of Genesis, the absence of any mention of Israel or the Law, all make the book look ancient – as well as the special uses of the names of God. Perhaps, Job was more of a Gentile than a Jew.

It is surprising therefore that Job uses another word in addition to Daysman, and perhaps he is the first in all Scripture to use it:

"I know that my redeemer liveth, and that he shall stand at the latter day upon the earth [dust]." (19:25)

Much as this section of scripture varies from one translation to another, indicating that the translators had some difficulty with the Hebrew, the essential message comes through:

"For I know that my Redeemer lives, and at last he will stand upon the earth; and after my skin has been thus destroyed, then from my flesh I shall see God, whom I shall see on my side, and my eyes shall behold, and not another." (RSV)

"I know that my Redeemer lives, and that in the end he will stand upon the earth. And after my skin has been destroyed, yet in my flesh I will see God; I myself will see him with my own eyes – I, and not another." (NIV)

The word redeemer is "*goel*", the word which occurs time and again as the kinsman who redeems. Job has moved from the daysman and sees something of his need, even though he has not yet seen God as totally right.

A Redeemer without a Daysman?

But does this mean that God will ignore the sin that the daysman would find in us and simply overlooks it without taking account of it? This is the whole problem at the heart of the atonement. The answer to the question is No, God does not simply ignore sin.

"Come now, and let us reason together, saith the LORD: though your sins be as scarlet, they shall be white as snow; though they be red like crimson, they shall be

171

as wool. If ye be willing and obedient ..."

(Isaiah 1:18,19)

The word "reason" is daysman, and by this means our sins are made manifest. But God is not going to press the umpire's case to its ultimate conclusion ("the soul that sinneth it shall die"). Instead He is to provide forgiveness, an option which Job had not perceived in its fulness. This is the essence of the nature of the Lord God who is merciful and gracious.

The Answer in Zechariah 3

The answer to Job's problem is revealed in Zechariah 3, among other passages. The events in the chapter took place in the second year of Darius, the year when the rebuilding of the temple was recommenced after the Jews' adversaries had been rebuked by the king.

In this setting where Jerusalem has its adversary (Satan), his attacks are to be silenced and a High Priest is to stand up who shall serve in the temple of the Lord.

We might have satisfied ourselves that the picture was wholly appropriate to the time of Zechariah and passed on. However, we are arrested in our tracks when we are told that the scene is really about something greater, about "My servant the BRANCH".

Joshua represents Christ, who is the Branch, the Stone, the Servant of the Lord God who will "remove the iniquity of that land in one day" (verse 9).

This is none other than the Lord Jesus presented to us in filthy garments and then transformed by a change of raiment and a fair mitre. He who shared our nature and bore away our sins is portrayed first in the old garments. This is entirely appropriate and the only way in which both the daysman and the redeemer could be set forth.

"Behold, there was none of you that convinced Job" (Job 32:12) contrasts with "Which of you convinceth me of sin" (John 8:46). The word "convinced" is daysman in Job. The word used in the Septuagint translation of Job 32:12 reappears in John 8:46. Christ was the only one who could bear the scrutiny of the daysman; and yet he was the one to be the Redeemer.

It is one of those happy coincidences of our daily readings that Zechariah 3 is referred to in our third reading for the day, Jude:

"Others save with fear, pulling them out of the fire; hating even the garment spotted by the flesh."

(verses 22,23 – see Zechariah 3:1-4)

This passage makes very clear our position in the sight of God. However righteous our lives may appear in our own sight, or even in the estimation of others, every human being (with the exception of the Lord) soils his character by sin. Like Job, we need the offices of a redeemer who has been assessed by the divine daysman. Jude therefore ends with a cry of triumphant praise:

"Now unto him that is able to keep you from falling, and to present you faultless before the presence of his glory with exceeding joy, to the only wise God our Saviour [through Christ Jesus our Lord RV], be glory and majesty, dominion and power, both now and ever. Amen"

(verses 24,25)

31

YEAR'S END
31st December

Job 41,42 **Malachi 3,4** **Revelation 21,22**

THE year is rolling relentlessly toward its close. Some of us have seen the passing of many similar periods and some of us comparatively few; but most of us experience an almost indefinable sighing of the spirit as the last grains of the year-glass run out. It is especially so in northern climes where the dying year draws the sun away with it and leaves us but shrunken days and swollen nights.

A year is a God-given period of time. The earth completes its great circuit in almost exactly that length of time. It is, perhaps, this annual birth and death of time which causes us to review our life, to take stock of our spiritual wares and to determine to buy and sell only at wisdom's gates as a new year stretches before us.

Nebuchadnezzar

One has only to look through the Bible with these thoughts in mind to find many apt words of exhortation. Has our year been like Nebuchadnezzar's? A profitable year so far as material things are concerned with ambitions achieved and satisfaction in accomplishment? If such is the case, and it is sure to be so for some of us, let us approach the year's end with thanksgiving to the giver of every good and perfect gift.

In this Babylon's king failed. He strutted in the royal palace "at the end of twelve months", perhaps even strolled through the great hanging gardens, and he made the mistake of the godless: "Is not this great Babylon that I have built … ?" A royal year could have been placed at the feet of the King of heaven, but it slipped through mortality's sieve. "Man that is in honour, and understandeth not, is like the beasts …". Shall we not take the fleeting years, therefore, and render them eternal by placing them in the hands of the Ancient of Days? By so doing each one will become an acceptable year of the Lord.

Time spent Wisely

This message is the more urgent as we learn one of the great lessons of our life in the Truth – our utter poverty without God. Without Him we have nothing of permanence. Our passing days are traded for transient things. We spend our years, says the word, and what will there be to show for it at the end? It is a wise man who takes himself to the eternal and unchangeable God in good time, declaring in faith and hope: "My times are in thy hand". To travel with God day by day is worth more than a lifetime of self-drive journeying.

When the Egyptians stood before Joseph in the time of famine we read: "When that year was ended, they came unto him ... and said unto him, We will not hide it from my lord, how that all our money is spent ...". So, too, our allotment of days will come to an end. We shall not be able to hide it from men or from God. The only consolation will lie in a proper answer to the question: 'How did you spend your time?'

The Bible Companion

There is, however, one sweet blessing which each year brings. It is the Bible Companion. We launch forth in January upon Genesis, Psalms and Matthew in fair winds and with a good heart. In December we are buffeted by the winds of Job, Zechariah and Revelation and, occasionally, look at our compass in bewilderment! But as the last days of the year fall away we sail into harbour with the rising sun. There we see "the end of the LORD, that the LORD is very pitiful, and of tender mercy"; there we see the company of those who have "feared the LORD and spake often one to another"; and there is the Lamb's book of life and the throne of God. Could any year end more hopefully? Does not this unique system of Bible reading which most of us follow, more or less, ensure that we see the years as part of the great purpose? Is it not the perfect way of looking with God upon the land of promise, for His eyes are upon it "from the beginning of the year even unto the end of the year"?

Lessons of the Year

One of the strangest yearly events we find in the pages of our reading is the annual weighing ceremony. It was the ritual of Absalom's haircutting:

"For it was at every year's end that he polled it ... he weighed the hair of his head at two hundred shekels after the king's weight." (2 Samuel 14:26)

Obviously he could not help this wondrous growth which fills many of us with envy, but, quite clearly, it had become a matter of personal vanity. By a strange irony it is almost certain that it was party to his death when he hung by his head from the great oak in the wood of Ephraim. Poor Absalom! A king's son, a beloved son, yet ruined by ambition and self-esteem. The warning is as clear as a beacon on the hilltop. Pride is as deadly as the serpent's fang. All his charms – and he had many – were gifts from God and could have been used in the Lord's service. None of them was evil in itself. That which had come by the accident of birth could have been acknowledged before the God of David his father. Absalom was able to weigh his hair after the king's weight but he could not count its myriad silken strands. Our Heavenly Father has made it a matter of assurance and promise by His power in the fiery furnace with Daniel's faithful friends, for there was not a hair of their heads singed. Also through His word in Jesus our Lord, that the very hairs of our head are all numbered such that, if we trust Him to the end, not one of them shall perish.

Absalom's self-assessment was worthless. Two hundred shekels after the king's weight! There was a greater King who could both number and weigh. "God hath numbered thy kingdom, and finished it ... thou art weighed in the balances, and art found wanting." How shall we stand at our year's end? Only the King's weight will have any significance. "The LORD is a God of knowledge, and by him actions are weighed."

The King's Son

There was another King's son, the beloved, the promised son of David, who came to Jerusalem. His head was not proud or lifted up and he did not seek the throne saying "Oh that I were made judge in the land". The favour of the

177

people was not his, for they greeted him with shame and spitting, and he gave his cheek to them that plucked off the hair. There was prepared for him a tree, not for his pride or self-esteem, but for the deliverance of his people. This was his final year. His lifetime seemed to have withered, his days were shortened, and some thought that he was another of the sons of men to be borne away on the stream of time, another who had miscalculated and failed. But it was not so. He who ripens the year's harvest, giving bread to the eater and seed to the sower, took that final year of our Lord and "crowned it with his goodness". Those few withered years are passed and have been replaced by the years of God's right hand. He is now the Son for evermore, his days are without end. The face of the man of sorrows is changed, and the God of all grace and comfort "hath made everything beautiful in his time".

The Ingathering

There is another thought here. Agriculturally the year ends when all the fruits of the season have been gathered in. This was the time of Israel's third great feast: the feast of ingathering, "in the end of the year, when thou hast gathered in thy labours out of the field". This was a feast of thanksgiving and rejoicing, the purpose and promise of the year were fulfilled. The families of Israel tabernacled around the holy city and celebrated the unfailing goodness of God. Hearts and voices swelled with praise and the priesthood relayed their joy to heaven. No one was empty handed – how could he be when God had given him good measure, pressed down and running over?

God, the great Sower, is waiting for that day. The promise of the harvest is in Jesus made glorious; it will yield more sheaves in the great day of his coming, and the harvest carts will be fully laden when the kingdom is delivered up to the Father.

Such are some of the lessons of the year. Shall we then bring our year to the feet of our Lord? In him alone will all our mingled feelings find rest. Companions lost or found, days when the year has smiled upon us and frowned upon us, our strivings and failings – all will find meaning in him if we so desire it.

The Son is our Clock

The sun is the clock. It marks our hours, our days and years. It is the centre around which our earth makes a majestic and faithful yearly journey. But the Son is *our* clock. By him we measure our days and years. We count time from his coming and to his second coming. He is the great Today if we will hear his voice. He is the ever-living invitation to look beyond each passing day to a risen and perfect Christ who shares the Father's endless days. With them that word is true which says "Thy years shall not fail", "Thy years are throughout all generations". If this Son is the centre of our yearly circuit, and if we seek not to grieve him in our flight, then the days of the years of our pilgrimage will be eternally remembered.

Before there was ever a sun, there was God. God measures not time by the sun: the sun is measured by Him. He is the centre of all creation, outside all created time and timepieces. And that is beyond our understanding. It is significant to notice, however, that the city of God that shall be has no need of the light of the sun or the light of the moon. This has primarily a spiritual meaning, of course. It has also a literal meaning, perhaps. Those who are counted worthy to attain unto that world and the life to come, will have no need of solar or of lunar years, for, having stood in their lot at the end of the days, they will be made like unto the Son of God after the power of an endless life.

179